Explaining the Faith Series

UNDERSTANDING DIVINE MERCY

by Fr. Chris Alar, MIC

MARIAN PRESS
STOCKBRIDGE   MA 01263

Available from:
Marian Helpers Center
Stockbridge, MA 01263
Prayerline: 1-800-804-3823
Orderline: 1-800-462-7426
Websites: TheDivineMercy.org
marian.org

Library of Congress Catalog Number: 2020925345
ISBN: 978-1-59614-539-9
Publisher: Marian Press
Publication date: February 15, 2021

Imprimi Potest
Very Rev. Kazimierz Chwalek, MIC
Provincial Superior
The Blessed Virgin Mary, Mother of Mercy Province
December 21, 2020

Nihil Obstat
Dr. Robert A. Stackpole, STD
Censor Deputatus
December 21, 2020

"Oh, how great is the goodness of God, greater than we can understand. There are moments and there are mysteries of the Divine Mercy over which the heavens are astounded. Let our judgment of souls cease, for God's mercy upon them is extraordinary"

(*Diary of Saint Maria Faustina Kowalska*, 1684).

CREATION
REDEMPTION
DIVINIZATION
SANCTIFICATION

Contents

~ FOREWORD ~

When people ask me why is the message of Divine Mercy important for the world today, the answer is simple: Through the message of Divine Mercy, our Lord is preparing us for His final coming.

He makes clear in Scripture that when He returns He's not going to deal with sin, because He's done that once and for all. When He comes again, it's "to bring salvation to those who eagerly await Him" (Heb 9:28, NABRE).

He told the great prophet of Divine Mercy, St. Maria Faustina, in one of a series of revelations in the 1930s: **"Mankind will not have peace until it turns with trust to My Mercy"** (*Diary of Saint Maria Faustina Kowalska*, 300). Helena Kowalska, known today throughout the world as St. Maria Faustina (1905-38), was designated by our Lord Himself as the "Secretary" and "Apostle" of His Mercy. The Lord told her: **"You will prepare the world for My final coming"** (*Diary*, 429).

The mission the Lord gave her was not only to remind the world of the great mercy of God as revealed in Sacred Scripture, but also to teach us new forms of devotion to the Divine Mercy and to initiate a movement of apostles of the Divine Mercy who show a childlike trust in God and love of neighbor.

For anyone interested in joining this movement — and I pray that includes all of you who are reading this — this book by Fr. Chris Alar, MIC, provides a perfect entry point.

But before turning it over to Fr. Chris, I just wish to say a few things.

The first concerns "private revelations." Indeed, the Divine Mercy devotion was given by the Lord to the world through St. Faustina and is what the Church calls "private revelation." (Note: the message of Divine Mercy is from Scripture and is what the Church calls "public revelation," the term given for the revealing action of God directed to humanity as expressed in the Old and New Testaments.) So what are we to make of Church-approved "private revelation?" Well, it's important to remember what St. Paul said. He said the Church is built on the foundation of the apostles and prophets (see Eph 2:19-22). Then St. Augustine and St. Thomas after him identify the prophets of the Church as the people who receive private revelations.

But why does God resort to private revelations? Father Karl Rahner, SJ, the German theologian writing about private revelations, said that all the mysteries of the Church, taken together, cannot be emphasized all at once — and to the same degree. So from time to time, he says, the Holy Spirit puts a spotlight on a particular mystery that the Church and the world need to pay special attention to at a given time.

The revelations of the Divine Mercy are both public and private revelation and are thus particularly tailored to our times. But don't just take my word for it. Pope Saint John Paul II clearly took these revelations seriously. In 1981 he wrote an entire encyclical dedicated to the Divine Mercy entitled *Dives in Misericordia* (*Rich in Mercy*), illustrating that the heart of the mission of Jesus Christ was to reveal the merciful love of the Father. In 1993, he beatified Sr. Faustina. In 1997, at Blessed Faustina's tomb in Lagiewniki, Poland, he proclaimed: "There is nothing that man needs more than Divine Mercy. ... From here went out the message of Mercy that Christ Himself chose to pass on to our generation through Blessed Faustina." In 2000 he canonized St. Faustina, the first canonized saint of the new millennium, and on that same day he also established "Divine Mercy Sunday" as a special title for the Octave Sunday of Easter for the universal Church.

In his homily on Divine Mercy Sunday in 2001, Pope John Paul II called the revelations given to St. Faustina "The appropriate and incisive answer that God wanted to offer to the questions and expectations of human beings in our time, marked by terrible tragedies. ... Divine Mercy! This is the Easter gift that the Church receives from the risen Christ and offers to humanity at the dawn of the third millennium."

Later, in Lagiewniki, Poland in 2002, the Holy Father said: "I wish solemnly to entrust the world to the Divine Mercy. I do so with the burning desire that the message of God's merciful love, proclaimed here through St. Faustina, may be made known to all the peoples of the earth and fill their hearts with hope. May this message radiate from this place to our beloved homeland and throughout the world." Then, with direct allusion to our Lord's statement to St. Faustina, and quoting the last part of it, the Holy Father declared: "May the binding promise of the Lord Jesus be fulfilled: From here there must go forth 'the spark which will prepare the world for His final coming' (*Diary*, 1732). This spark needs to be lighted by the grace of God. This fire of mercy needs to be passed on to the world. In the mercy of God; the world will find peace and mankind will find happiness!"

Why did St. Pope John Paul II so strongly recommend that we pay heed to the Divine Mercy message and devotion? Clearly, he did so because he saw it as more than just a collection of "private revelations"; rather, he saw them as prophetic revelations. In other words, revelations given to us by God to proclaim the heart of the Gospel in a way especially suited to meet the needs of our era.

Now, 116 years have passed since our dear saint's birth on Aug. 25, 1905. And each Oct. 5, we mark her departure from this earth to take the place destined for her, close to God. However, we who wish to stand ready and "eagerly await Him" should not forget her promise to us: "Poor earth, I will not forget you," she wrote. "Although I feel that I will be immediately drowned in God as in an ocean of happiness, that will not be an obstacle to my returning to earth to encourage souls and incite them to trust in God's mercy. Indeed, this immersion in God will give me the possibility of boundless action" (*Diary*, 1582).

May this book by Fr. Chris lead us to drawing ever deeper into St. Faustina's life and writings. May we learn to count on St. Faustina's promised help in order to bring about what our Lord so much desires from us and needs from us. May we be inspired to have boundless trust in Him who is the unfailing Divine Mercy in Person.

— Fr. Seraphim Michalenko, MIC
January 1, 2021

Father Seraphim Michalenko, MIC, served as vice-postulator for North America in St. Maria Faustina's canonization cause.

~ CHAPTER ONE ~

What is
Divine Mercy?

As Fr. Seraphim Michalenko, MIC, is fond of saying, "The Divine Mercy message and devotion is the largest grassroots movement in the history of the Catholic Church." And the Marian Fathers of the Immaculate Conception (MICs) and our Marian Helpers have been at the heart of it since 1941, hardly three years after the death of St. Maria Faustina Kowalska, the Lord's "secretary" of Divine Mercy. We are a religious community that has been specifically entrusted by God and the Church to teach the world about this important revelation.

In 2001, the 60th anniversary of the Marians' involvement in the spread of Divine Mercy, Pope St. John Paul II sent a special apostolic blessing and a renewed call to the Marian Fathers when he said: "Be apostles of Divine Mercy under the maternal and loving guidance of Mary." Inspired by this "Great Mercy Pope," we continue our task in the third millennium to make it known that, in the words of Jesus to St. Faustina, **"Mankind will not have peace until it turns with trust to My Mercy"** (*Diary of Saint Maria Faustina Kowalska*, 300). We believe there is no more important work in the world that we Marians could be doing right now, and we believe there is no more important topic in the world you could be reading about right now.

My religious congregation and I tirelessly spread this important message and devotion, and most of our work begins on the grounds of the National Shrine of The Divine Mercy in Stockbridge, Massachusetts (you may recognize our Shrine as the place where the Chaplet of Divine Mercy — recited daily on EWTN — was recorded). It's a beautiful location, perfectly suited to greeting pilgrims who come here. And this brings up a question: Why do people visit shrines, or any church for that matter? It is because these are the places where, in a special and intimate way, we can encounter Jesus through prayer and the Sacraments.

So who is this *Jesus?* This may seem like a basic question to some, but there's more to it than you might think.

I believe all Christians can agree that Jesus is the Incarnate Second Person of the Holy Trinity (one God in three persons). However, if I asked you to please give me one word that best describes God, what word would that be? The most applicable descriptor would be *love*. God is love (see 1 Jn 4:16).

But why love? There are many virtues or attributes of God that we could apply to Him. We could say God is *omnipotent* because He's all powerful. We could say God is *omniscient* because He's all knowing. But why do we think of God first as love? The answer lies in the virtues that animate the Christian life and define its character. Of all the virtues, and there are many — including justice, prudence, fortitude, patience, faith, hope, among others — the greatest of these is love! (See 1 Cor 13:13.) We associate God with love because it is the most supreme of all virtues.

But as the Greeks taught us, not all love is the same. For example, there is romantic love (*eros*), there is love between a father and a son (*filial* love), and there is an even higher form of love, *agape* love, which is a complete giving of one's self. Each of these modes of love has its own distinctions. To illustrate, I got my master of business administration degree from the University of Michigan, and I have always loved Michigan college football. But, do I love Michigan football in the same way I love my mom? She probably would say "yes!" But of course, that's not true.

We have different modes of love, but the greatest mode of love is *mercy*. Mercy is the highest form of the highest virtue — you can't do better. If you want to get to Heaven, the surest and best way is to be merciful as the heavenly Father is merciful (see Lk 6:36). Accept God's mercy and return it to your neighbor. Love God, and love your neighbor. These are the two greatest commandments given to us by Christ Himself. Of all the virtues, the greatest is love. And of all the modes of love, the highest is mercy.

To elaborate further, mercy is the particular mode of love that leads to action. For instance, when this mode of love encounters suffering, it seeks to alleviate that suffering. Now, what do I mean by that? We have all come across those images shown on late-night television of starving children and the victims of natural disasters. We often say to ourselves, "Oh, that's too bad, somebody needs to do something about that!" And then we continue our channel surfing. Here we have missed an opportunity to live mercy — that is to say, to recognize suffering, take it into our heart, and take action to do something about it. We can live mercy by doing something as great as physically going to the disaster area to assist, or we can live mercy by doing something as simple as just praying a short prayer at that very moment.

Either way, we are exercising mercy. While there are many ways we can practice mercy, Jesus told St. Faustina that He gives us three specific ways to do so: in words, in deeds, and in prayer (see *Diary*, 742). We have no excuses for not being merciful, since Christ commands it and since we can all carry out at least one of these commands in any given situation.

One of the great teachers of Divine Mercy and a friend of our Marian Community, the late Fr. George Kosicki, CSB, would say, "Mercy is having pain in your heart for the pain of another and taking pains to do something about their pain." Now that's a lot of pain, but we all experience pain in some way and we all share in the pain of our friends and loved ones in some fashion. In other words, we are all suffering.

Did God Create Evil?

Obviously, there is a significant amount of suffering and evil in the world today. Just watch the daily news and within five minutes, you will have had a full dose of it. One such example, school shootings, seemed to dominate the national news for months on end. While the seemingly endless string of tragedies never directly affected me, I saw the devastating affect they had on many people over the years.

One such instance occurred when I spoke at a parish mission in Tuscola, Illinois, in 2019. After my talk, a gentleman approached me and said, "Father, my niece is a student at Parkland High School. That's where the horrible Florida high school shooting occurred last year. You know, Father, for a year, she struggled. She lost 17 friends that day." After a moment of speechlessness, I uttered, "I'm so sorry to hear that." But I wasn't ready for what he was about to say next.

With his voice shaking, he said, "Father, Monday *she* took her life." At that moment I felt all of the energy inside me being sucked out. All I could do was return a stare of compassion in his direction and place my hand on his shoulder. Then he softly said, "Well Father, two days after she took her life, another student took their life." I was discouraged to learn that two more people had now died needlessly in the wake of this calamity. It was a tragedy of the greatest proportions. He then expressed his confusion as to how God could allow such evil.

To answer this age-old question, let me ask you two questions: First, does evil exist as a real, created thing? Second, did God create it? The answer to both is "no." But one may refer to the Florida shooting and say, "There you go, evil is everywhere, and since God created everything, he created evil itself and now we have to deal with it."

Actually, evil is not *something*, it is a *lack* of something. Evil is a privation — or lack — of the good. God by His very nature is *Goodness* itself, so when we remove God from our schools, from our courts, from our families, from the whole of society, we are removing Goodness itself. And what is left? A privation of the good. That is the very definition of evil — a lack of the good. Because God's very nature is goodness, He can't act in any way contrary to the good, so He cannot create evil. Evil is explained by the realization that when we remove what is good from our society, there are consequences that result in the occurrence of evil.

I recall seeing a T-shirt in the airport a few years ago. It referenced other school shootings in bold lettering as it stated: "Columbine, Sandy Hook ... God, how can you let this happen in our schools?" The line below was God's response: "I'm not allowed in your schools!" Because of this removal of God (Goodness itself) from our lives, resulting in the embrace of secular ideals and sinfulness, we are inflicting more sufferings upon ourselves. And the effects are seen both privately and communally. When we sin, we don't just affect our own lives and the fate of our own soul — we inject a kind of poison (so to speak) into the world, damaging the goodness of God's creation. This may very well be why we have so many hurricanes, earthquakes, and tsunamis, because every time we sin, we bring disharmony into God's universe.

The Consequences of Sin and God's Response

When the allure of sin presents itself to us, we should avoid taking for granted God's mercy and the danger of flippantly saying to ourselves, "I can give in to this temptation, because it doesn't hurt anyone else and I can just run to Confession tomorrow." While it is true that our sins are forgiven in the confessional (as long as we have a valid Confession), unless we have perfect contrition, which is contrition that arises purely out of love of God rather than fear of punishment, our Confession doesn't necessarily make everything automatically disappear. There are consequences to our sins that may remain, even after those sins we confessed have been forgiven.

After all, when we sin we don't just harm ourselves — we scar the entire Body of Christ. And as we noted above, those scars may remain even after the wound of sin

is healed in Confession. Unless all of our sins are forgiven
and atoned for (through such acts as penances, fasting,
additional prayers, etc.), then temporal punishment due to
sin may remain on our souls. This is because the justice of
God still requires satisfaction, or atonement. Although this
"punishment" can be better understood as God's loving and
Fatherly discipline, it requires that we endure some form of
suffering, either in this life or in Purgatory after this life.

There is hope, however. God knows we are suffering
as a result of our sins, and He wants to help. He knows
we are broken, and He wants to do something about it.
This is the definition of mercy (love encountering suffering
and taking action to do something about it) and when this
mercy applies to God, it is known as *Divine Mercy*. God
loves us, and He wants to forgive and heal us. He wants to
have mercy on us.

Father Seraphim's definition of mercy expounds on
this concept. He states mercy is "loving the unlovable
and forgiving the unforgivable." Are we unlovable? If we
consider our sins in the natural order of things, yes. Are
we unforgivable? Naturally speaking, yes. What we've done
— sin — is the worst crime because it's a crime against the
infinite love of God. That is why St. Paul tells us we deserve
the worst kind of punishment. He says, "The wages of sin
is death" (Rom 6:23, RSVCE). So if sin brings us nothing
but suffering and death, how do we find a way out of this
mess we got ourselves into? What is the "medicine" for this
condition? What is the remedy for our suffering?

The answer is found in *Divine Mercy*, which is essentially defined as *God* loving the unlovable and forgiving
the unforgivable. By our sins we have made ourselves both
technically unlovable and unforgivable, and as a result, we
suffer terribly. It is in Divine Mercy, given to us by God,
through the Church (the Mystical Body of Christ) that we
find the answer.

The Ultimate Remedy: The Mass

God gave us the remedy for our suffering in His Church, and most specifically in the *Mass*. The Liturgy is indispensable for growth in our spiritual life, yet few people understand that, or worse, outright reject it. We all know someone who says, "I am not into organized religion. I don't need the four walls of a church; I don't need Mass because I pray in the privacy of my own room."

This is understandable up to a point. Scripture tells us, "Go into your room and shut the door and pray" (Mt 6:6, RSVCE). While indispensable, that form of prayer is just the start, because when we pray on our own, it's like learning to walk — our private prayer is imperfect. Why? Because we're all broken. We're all sinful, and those sins are like shades over the windows of that very same room we go into to pray in private. God's grace, like the sun, is always shining; it's trying to penetrate through those "shades" on the windows of our souls. However, just as much of that light gets blocked by the shades on our windows, much of God's grace is blocked by the darkness of our sins. Our private prayer is great, but because we are sinful (even if we are in a state of grace), our broken human nature makes all of our prayers less than perfect.

Thus, even though our private prayer is virtuous and needed, it's not sufficient on its own. So where is perfect prayer found? It is found in the religion Jesus established, called the Catholic Church. Specifically, it is found in the Mass. Why? As Fr. Edmund McCaffrey, the former abbot of Belmont Abbey, located near Charlotte, North Carolina, used to say, "The Mass is *God* offering *God* to *God*." Anything that God offers is perfect, and in the Mass, we see the perfect worship offered to the Father, by the Son, through the Holy Spirit.

It is in the Mass that we witness God's grand plan of salvation history play out before our eyes. We witness a pattern of *exitus et reditus*, of going out and returning. I will discuss this in more detail in the next few sections. But for now, suffice to say, this Latin term roughly translates to "All comes from God; all will return to God." God the Son comes forth from the Trinity to the world first through the covenants He established with man and then ultimately through the Incarnation (*exitus*), and He then returns home to the Father as the Lamb who is slain (*reditus*).

However, there is one huge difference when He returns: Jesus now is carrying us on His shoulders like the shepherd carries his discovered lost sheep back home to safety. Jesus is returning to the Father, but He is now bringing us in our redeemed humanity with Him. We were broken after the fall of Adam and Eve, but we are now being healed and sanctified. After Christ's redemptive act on the Cross, He draws us all to Him through the Sacraments, offering us His very Body and Blood that was shed for us as the penalty for our sins.

Remember, we learn from St. Paul that the penalty for sin is death. Jesus has paid that penalty and then resurrected to defeat death so that we can now have life in Him. That is one of the main reasons Jesus died on the Cross: He paid the ultimate debt so that if we are united with Him, we don't have to. Not only does Christ save us from this fate of eternal death by dying for us on the Cross, He has resurrected to defeat physical death so that it no longer has any hold over us. He returns to the Father as an offering for us, having wed His divinity to our humanity, and He elevates us to share in the Divine Life of the Trinity! During the Mass, through the power of the Holy Spirit, we are present when Christ makes this offering of Himself, wedded to us, back to the Father, in atonement for our sins and the sins of the whole world.

If you come to Mass and listen attentively, to whom are the prayers of the Mass addressed to? Most people would answer, "Jesus." But the answer is really the *Father*. Who is addressing those prayers to the Father? Jesus. So is Jesus reading from the missal? No, the priest is. That priest is acting *in persona Christi*, in the Person of Christ. He's an *alter Christus*, another Christ. This substitution enables the true sacrifice to be made.

Many people ask what the "high point" of the Mass is. Most would answer, "the Consecration." Others, such as St. Maximilian Kolbe, would say that the high point of the Mass is when we receive Holy Communion.[1] But if you've read Fr. Michael Gaitley's *The One Thing is Three* (and some theologians agree with him), the high point of the Mass, the "supercharged moment," is the part the Church calls the "Concluding Doxology."

The Concluding Doxology is the prayer uttered when the priest, in the person of Christ, takes the paten and the chalice and elevates them, saying, "Through him, and with him, and in him, O God, almighty Father, in the unity of the Holy Spirit, all glory and honor is yours, for ever and ever." What is going on here? God the Son is being offered, through the power of the Holy Spirit, to God the Father, in complete self-sacrificial love.

It should be noted that Christ is not just a passive participant in this offering. He is the One offering and the One being offered, all through the power of the Holy Spirit. Why does that Sacrifice have to be offered? Again, the penalty for sin is death, but now Christ is paying that debt. In fact, because God is outside of time (there is no past or future for God, but according to St. Thomas Aquinas, there is only one "eternal present moment" for God),[2] you are actually there at Calvary in a mystical way as Jesus is paying the "death penalty" for your sin. That is why at every Catholic Mass, there is a crucifix on the altar bearing the Body of Christ.

You are not at a play or the acting out of a dramatic event in human history; you are actually there for the most dramatic event ever witnessed in human history. You are

at the foot of the Cross as Jesus dies in your place to pay
the debt you could not pay so you could be free and have
eternal life. Mass is not an act *representing* the Sacrifice of
Christ, it is a *re-presentation* of the Sacrifice of Christ and we
are active participants in this ultimate Sacrifice. That is why
we must do more than just "be present" at Mass — we need
to actively participate!

In his book *The Spirit of the Liturgy*, Cardinal Joseph
Ratzinger (the future Pope Benedict XVI) states that at the
Mass, Heaven and earth are connected as at no other time.
The angels and saints ascend and descend, and "sacred
time" (God's time) is united with "physical time" (our
time). At Mass, you are spiritually present at Calvary when
the one sacrifice of Christ for the salvation of mankind is
occurring.[3] Although you are physically present in a church
pew in the 21st century, you are spiritually present at the
greatest moment ever, not just in the last 2,000 years, but
since time began!

Ratzinger explains:

> Now if past and present penetrate one another in
> this way, if the essence of the past is not simply
> a thing of the past but the far-reaching power
> of what follows in the present, then the future,
> too, is present in what happens in the liturgy …
> Past, present, and future interpenetrate and touch
> upon eternity.[4]

The Mass is so consequential, so eternally significant,
that all of creation is present for this moment. That is why
our Guardian Angels rejoice when their wards physically
attend Mass, because there they also can participate in this
perfect worship of God in Heaven. The mystics tell us that
our Guardian Angels all come and kneel around the altar at
the moment of Consecration, holding vessels. And what is
in those vessels? What you put into them: your hopes, your

joys, your suffering, your pain, etc. This is the offering that will soon be united with Christ on the Cross and offered back to the Father by the power of the Holy Spirit during the Concluding Doxology. Now you can understand why your private prayers are good, but these prayers united with the perfect Sacrifice of the Son to the Father are *perfect*.

The Wedding Feast

This incredible reality goes even deeper, into a nuptial meaning. The early Church Fathers often described the Mass as a marriage of Christ to His Bride, the Church (us), in the heavenly Wedding Feast of the Lamb. You may be asking yourself, "Father, why would this be, aren't I already married to my one true spouse for all eternity? His name is Frank." Remember, when you were married to your spouse, you were married in earthly terms. But will there be "marriage" in this same way in Heaven? No. Jesus tells us there will be no marriage in Heaven (see Mt 22:30). While this may make some people sad (and sadly make some others happy!), let's look at why this is so.

Hopefully, you already know the three "objectives" of marriage. One is *procreation*, which includes being open to life and having children, the fruit of the love shared between spouses. There doesn't need to be procreation in Heaven, because there is no longer any death; everyone in Heaven will live for all eternity.

The second objective of marriage is *union*. Spouses share in the incredible gift of the conjugal act, where two people "become one flesh" (Mk 10:8, NABRE) and there is a renewal of God's covenant. On earth you are united with your spouse in a special way, but in Heaven, you'll be united with Love itself, with God, in an even more intimate way. There will no longer be a need for sexual relations in Heaven, because there will no longer be a need to procreate, and there we will have ultimate union with God.

The third and most critically important objective of marriage is for you and your spouse, through the lifelong practice of mutual love, to help each other *get to Heaven*. This means accepting the good with the bad, so the next time you see the one you married as being a "cross," rejoice! That is because we can only enter Heaven by way of the Cross, and sometimes the crosses our loved ones make us bear are God's way of purifying us, sanctifying us, and raising us in virtue so we can inherit eternal life by surrendering our will in a powerful, self-sacrificial way. Like the other two, this objective is not needed in Heaven because your spouse is either there with you or not for all eternity (we pray for the former).

Thus, there is no need for marriage in Heaven in the same way we know it here on earth because you'll have the ultimate marriage in Heaven, to the ultimate Spouse — God Himself. In a powerful way, however, God gives us a foretaste of this right here on earth: The Wedding Feast of the Lamb — the Mass. In the Mass, God unites with us in the most intimate way possible while still on earth.

In Scripture, Christ often refers to Himself as the "bridegroom," for example, in the parable of the Ten Virgins (see Mt 25:1-13). Elsewhere in Scripture, Jesus is questioned about why He and His disciples aren't fasting. He replies, "Can the wedding guests mourn as long as the bridegroom is with them? The days will come, when the bridegroom is taken away from them, and then they will fast" (Mt 9:15, RSVCE). Many of the Church Fathers have described this incredible love shared by Christ, the Bridegroom, with His Bride, the Church.

At every Mass, when you walk up the aisle of the Church to receive Holy Communion, you can think of it as your wedding march. In every Catholic wedding, when the beautiful bride processes up the aisle, who's waiting for her at the altar? Her groom. He sees the most beautiful spouse he could ever imagine coming toward him. In the Sacrament of Matrimony, the two then become one; they're spiritually united at the altar. After the wedding, the marriage is consummated when the groom literally enters into the bride and the two "become one flesh."

In an even deeper way, when you go to the foot of the altar at Mass, you meet your spouse, Christ, who is literally waiting for you in the flesh. In this most intimate and supernatural union, as the true Bridegroom enters into you, the Bride, in Holy Communion, your union with Christ is consummated!

This is the meaning of the Mass! It's a holy nuptial. It's beautiful. Mass isn't just about coming to stand, sit, and kneel. Mass is about coming to engage in this most incredible mystery. What makes the Catholic Church different from every other religion in the world are the Sacraments. The Sacraments aren't just symbols. They are a means by which God dispenses His love, His mercy. In other words, they do something! The Sacraments "do" what they symbolize — they "confer the grace that they signify" (*Catechism of the Catholic Church*, 1127). As the *Catechism* tells us, the Sacraments are "efficacious signs of God's grace, instituted by Christ and entrusted to the Church, by which divine life is dispensed to us" (*Catechism*, 1131). You cannot get anything more incredible than that!

We have Holy Communion containing the Body, Blood, Soul and Divinity of Jesus, so that Christ can fully enter into us and live in us. If we are open to that grace and receive it worthily, it can be truly transformative — forming us into another *Christ*. That is what distinguishes us from our Protestant brethren, many of whom believe we are simply snow-covered "dung hills," and God's grace simply covers over us as we remain rotten at the core, so to speak. Catholics, on the other hand, believe God's grace truly transforms us — it sanctifies us and makes us holy. How does that happen? We shall now see.

God's Three Great Acts of Mercy

Our path to come home to God, the path established by God Himself, is through the Sacraments of the Catholic Church. Our whole faith can be summarized in a symbolic way as a *circle*. As mentioned earlier, that circle is what Thomas Aquinas called *"exitus et reditus."* In terms of salvation history, the circle of our faith progresses like this: Everything came from God (creation), but it became damaged after the fall in the Garden of Eden. Christ did the necessary fixing via His death on the Cross (redemption), and now ultimately we return to God repaired (sanctification).

Thus, we can now sum up all of God's acts of mercy into His *greatest acts of mercy*. In a way, we could call them God's "Greatest Hits Album," if I may be so crude as to explain this concept in popular terminology.

So, let's begin with God's first great act of mercy: *Creation.* I came from God, you came from God, we all came from God. Contemplating this awesome reality even more deeply, we see that we can attribute this *first* great act to the *First* Person of the Trinity: God the Father.

Sadly, it took man, the high point of God's creation, no time at all to get himself into trouble. Even though they were our parents, Adam and Eve were somewhat like your own children when you give them a new toy. Many times they'll break it within minutes, and that is exactly what happened in the Garden of Eden with the fall of man into sin.

Man, who was in a state of grace, lost his preternatural (spiritual) gifts and fell from grace, becoming "broken" and bringing about *concupiscence* — the constant tendency to now rebel against God and neighbor. This sin was a result of man taking his eyes off his Creator and focusing inward, not trusting in God, but rather only in himself (see *Catechism*, 397).[5] Now, instead of perfectly loving God and each other, Adam and Eve (and all humans who followed) had to bear the new reality of distrust, concupiscence, and brokenness.

Mankind was now in need of a Savior to rescue himself from this fallen condition.

This first sin brought about the need for God's second great act of mercy: *Redemption*. In this act of mercy, God had to intervene to fix the mess that man had made. A great chasm now existed between God and man that needed to be repaired. But we can see a great quandary: Since this relationship was broken by man, man should be the one to remedy it. However, it was such a deep divide that man was incapable of fixing it. This massive transgression was beyond his ability to reconcile; in reality, only God could fix it. Only God would be capable of healing the wound. But God didn't create the wound, so what to do? Answer: Jesus, both God and man, the *God-man*. To sum it up, God's first great act of mercy was to create us; then we got broken, so His *second* great act of mercy was to send His Son, the *Second* Person of the Trinity, to fix us. Jesus Christ redeemed us.

The key is for us to be properly disposed to let that gift of redemptive grace transform us, to be made holy as our heavenly Father is holy, so that we can fully share in the divine life of God. So, in the *third*, final, and in some ways greatest act of mercy, the *Third* Person of the Trinity, the Holy Spirit, came to sanctify us and make us holy so we could return to God the Father without stain or blemish. We call this third great act of mercy *divinization* or *sanctification*.[6]

Some people ask, "Father, when does our sanctification happen? At our Baptism?" Yes, in many ways. We're divinized at our Baptism, becoming "partakers of the divine nature" (see 1 Pet 3:21; 2 Pet 1:3-4, RSVCE), and thereby adopted sons and daughters of God. Some would say it happens when we die and enter into Heaven to behold the beatific vision. Yes, in many ways that is true, too. There, we behold the face of God Himself and fully share in the divine life of God for all eternity.

The Mass Further Explained

But where does this divinization happen every minute of every day, somewhere around the world? Answer: at the *Mass*. That's what is happening during the Consecration, during the Concluding Doxology, and when we receive Holy Communion. It is God's beautiful provision to make us holy, to sanctify us, through Christ's redeeming act. We return to the Father, from whom we came, in a much better state — a state full of grace. Wow! Partaking in this eternal sacrifice is the greatest thing you can ever do in your entire life! If we Catholics truly knew what was happening during the Mass, we would never miss Mass; we would never be bored at Mass; and we would be clamoring in excitement for the next opportunity to attend Mass!

This is why we need to be aware of the significance of being at Mass — being mystically present at Calvary as Christ is paying our debt on the Cross so that we can be sanctified and prepared to enter into divine life with our Creator. Through the Mass and the Sacraments, we are divinized and become sharers in God's divine life in the fullest way possible while on earth.

It frustrates me when I hear people complain, "Father, I don't go to Mass because I don't get anything out of it." I always reply, "How could you not get anything out of it? This is the grace you need for eternal life! Rather than being bored at Mass, put yourself prayerfully on that paten. Unite yourself with the offering of Jesus the Son to God the Father through the power of the Holy Spirit. Attach yourself to the Cross, even if you have to hold on to the bottom of it by Christ's feet as He returns to the Father in Heaven. Just don't miss this incredible gift Jesus is offering to you!"

This is the meaning of the Mass. The Church and her Sacraments are the ordinary means for Divine Mercy to work in the world, which is why the devil hates the Catholic

Church. He hates Catholic priests and works tirelessly to bring about their demise. He hates the Sacraments, and he especially hates Divine Mercy. Why? Because when we trust in Jesus and receive the Sacraments, especially Reconciliation and Holy Communion, we receive God's mercy in the fullest and most guaranteed way.

When we go to the Sacrament of Confession and receive absolution, there is no wondering, "*Am* I forgiven? *Maybe* I am forgiven? I *hope* I am forgiven!" You are guaranteed forgiveness or Jesus is a liar! (see Mt 16:19; Mt 18:18; Jn 20:23). Likewise, when you go to Holy Communion, there is no wondering, "Is this really Christ in the Eucharist? Does Jesus really dwell in me after receiving Holy Communion?" Again, if not, Jesus is a liar (see Jn 6:32-58), and nobody is going to claim that!

I often explain the importance of the Mass to my seventh-grade catechism class through an illustrative story. I tell the kids, "Guys, you're old enough to understand this, and hopefully none of you will ever be in this position, but I want you to think about something for a minute. What happens if you commit a terrible crime?" They all reply, "You get arrested." Then I say to them, "What happens next?" They always respond, "You go to jail." True, but they're forgetting something: You must first go before the judge.

Imagine you are going before God, the Just Judge, right now. That's how it will be at the end of your life, at your particular judgment. You will go before the throne of God, and, sorry, you will be all alone. You'll have no spouse, no son, daughter, mother, father, brother, or sister with you. You will be on your own. Then imagine how He can pull out your proverbial *rap sheet* that lists every little thing you have ever done right or wrong in your life.

This "Judge" has the right to hold you accountable for every infraction, every act of disobedience, and every omission in which you failed to act for the good of yourself and society — that means basically all of your sins. What could happen next is more intense than any courtroom drama found on television.

If you have confessed your sins, Satan (the prosecuting attorney) can't bring them up against you in condemnation during your time of trial. However, even Christ's atoning death cannot fully cover any sins that you have not completely repented of or are not deeply sorry for, meaning you have remained attached to them in some way. To make up for the effect of those sins, which have scarred the Body of Christ, you should have done penance and made reparation, maybe by fasting or offering little sacrifices of your own will. If you have not done that, purification will be required in Purgatory.

Unfortunately, many people will probably go before the judgment seat with *unconfessed* sin. Now this can get a little more serious. We are sinners, thus God has every right as the Just Judge to say: "Based on your rap sheet, you've committed the worst possible crime." As we said, the worst possible crime is sin, because it is a crime against God. That Judge could rightly look at you and say, "You've committed these horrible crimes. Your sentence is *death*." Yes, we all deserve the "death penalty" — and what is the ultimate death? Separation from God for all eternity in hell.

You (and all mankind) deserve to die for your crimes, eternally. But again, picture yourself in front of that Judge. You're sitting there. You're distraught. All of a sudden, the Judge steps down from the bench. He comes and stands next to you, and He gives you the most beautiful look of love. (Remember, I'm just giving you a seventh-grade analogy. This is not Church dogma.) The Judge says, "Be at peace My son; I will take your place. Do you accept My offer?" This is where our Protestant brothers and sisters have it right: You have to profess, "Yes, I accept You, Jesus Christ, as my personal Lord and Savior." This is the most incredible free gift of God, but we have to accept it in faith.

You can't simply reply, "Thanks, man. Sorry you have to go through all of that, but I'm out of here!" No, you have to accept this gift with your whole heart and soul. The Protestants nail this. But the problem is this is where they stop (many of them; of course, not all of them). Many of these wonderful non-Catholic brethren of ours proclaim, "That's it. That's all you have to do — simply profess Jesus as your personal Lord and Savior and you will be saved."

However, we Catholics believe differently. Yes, we need to receive the gift of faith through the saving love of Christ, but then we have to use it. We receive His sanctifying grace in our hearts in order to do authentic works of love — which, of course, further sanctify us! That's why St. Paul writes that nothing we do counts toward our final salvation except "faith working through love" (Gal 5:6, RSVCE).

Saint Paul tells us that faith without love (*works* in the Catholic sense) is nothing and it cannot save us (see 1 Cor 13:2). James 2:24-26 states, "You see that a man is justified by works and not by faith alone. ... For as the body apart from the spirit is dead, so faith apart from works is dead" (RSVCE). Here he is referring to "works of love," not works of the law.

To perform these works of love, we need to first accept God's love. Some people may not accept Jesus even in their final moments because they are not properly prepared to receive His mercy. Absent an extraordinary outpouring of grace, you die in the state you have lived. If you've been rejecting God your whole life, you may not be able to say "yes" to God's mercy at this critical moment, especially if you are not in a state of grace. This great need for God's grace at the hour of death is why we have to pray for those who died in a state of sin, and it underscores the importance of receiving the Sacraments in this life so that we can be in a state of grace when we die.

The Judge Doesn't Determine
Our Fate: We Do!

Now back to our scenario. There you are with this Just
Judge and He asks you, "Do you accept this offer of
mercy?" You reply, "Yes!" Who wouldn't? Now are you free
to go? Not exactly. The Judge is going to say to you, "Okay.
In order to work out the details, we need to meet again
Sunday morning at 8 a.m., 10 a.m., or 12:00 noon." You
know what I'm talking about — the Mass! This is where
we can do the greatest act of love — showing our love for
God, our Creator, by worshipping Him in the most perfect
way possible. But first, we must accept the perfect love He
is offering us.

It is at the Mass where we can "actively" accept this gift
of actual grace offered us, not just profess that we accept it.
Remember, Jesus said that "not every one who says to me,
'Lord, Lord,' shall enter the kingdom of heaven" (Mt 7:21,
RSVCE). This is the basis of Catholic teaching. You have a
choice. Either you can die eternally, or you can accept the
gift of Him who died for you. Which one do you want?
Jesus paid the penalty for *all* of us so all of us can choose to
accept that gift if we desire it.

Basically, Jesus is telling us the way to salvation is
through Him and through His offering at the Mass. Why?
Keeping in mind that the Mass is a wedding feast, and we
need to be present at our own wedding, another example
suffices to answer this question.

Recall the Wedding Feast in Matthew's Gospel (see Mt
22:1-14). In this parable, a king plans a banquet to celebrate
his son's wedding feast. He sends his servants to summon
those who have been invited, but they won't come (see Mt
22:1-3). He sends more servants to give them a second
chance, but they scoff at the invitation and go about their
pursuits, "one to his farm, another to his business" (Mt
22:4-5, RSVCE).

What happens next? The king decides that the guests he invited were not worthy of his generosity, so he sends his servants to go out into the streets and invite as many other people as they can find (see Mt 22:8-9). The ones originally invited have chosen to spurn the gift offered and end up being left out of everything altogether.

The lesson for us here is that we, especially baptized Catholics, are those invited guests. And when we choose our television, shopping, soccer practice, or football games ahead of attending Mass on Sunday, we are just like those men in the Gospel who declined the greatest gift ever offered so they could engage in worldly activities. The warning to not put our emphasis on the temporal, but rather on the eternal is found throughout Scripture.

We have been invited to the most beautiful wedding in the world. The worst thing we could ever choose to do is reject that invitation. If we do, at the end of our lives we could end up like the unfortunate people to whom Jesus says, "I do not know where you come from" (Lk 13:25, RSVCE). We could be shut out of Heaven, while those who have accepted His invitation to eternal life are enjoying His presence forever (see Lk 13:28).

Remember, Scripture tells us, "Every one to whom much is given, of him will much be required" (Lk 12:48, RSVCE). So don't turn down the most precious gift you will ever be offered. And don't fall into the trap of saying, "Then don't give it to me; I don't want that responsibility! Let me be like the ignorant people who don't know God and can still be saved, like the pygmy in the rainforest."

Unfortunately (or fortunately), it doesn't work that way. In today's modern world, especially in the West, few have any excuse for not knowing who Jesus is, so we won't be able to claim ignorance — nor should we want to. We should all be striving to come to know Christ, the very Source of love and mercy.

Why would we ever want to decline such an invitation? Go to the Mass, just like the Judge said, because at the Mass, you are experiencing a foretaste of Heaven. Even though Christ's Crucifixion occurred almost 2,000 years ago, you're there in a mystical way. This is your salvation. This is your ticket. God's mercy is seen most powerfully in the Mass; thus, we need to do whatever we can to attend, physically and spiritually.

We all know Christ instituted the Mass at the Last Supper. So what about all the people who lived before that time — did they receive God's mercy? Yes, Divine Mercy is present throughout salvation history. In fact, its presence in history goes back to the beginning of time and was even seen quite prevalently in the Garden of Eden.

Unlike Adam and Eve, Know Your ABCs!

When contemplating what Adam and Eve did to create such a mess for future generations, it is tempting (pun intended) to simply say, "They sinned." Yes, that is true. But as bad as that was, it wasn't the worst part. What happened *after* their fall into sin was perhaps more problematic.

First of all, did Adam and Eve ever *ask* for God's mercy and forgiveness after blatantly disobeying Him and eating from the tree of which they were forbidden? No, they didn't even say they were sorry or ask God for His forgiveness. Next, did they choose to *be merciful* to each other? No. In fact, Adam shifted the blame to Eve and even to God, sheepishly saying, "The woman whom thou gavest to be with me, she gave me fruit of the tree, and I ate" (Gen 3:12, RSVCE). As a result, husbands and wives have been blaming each other ever since! Finally, did they *trust* in God? No, they ran and hid from Him.

God could have justifiably crushed Adam and Eve out of existence and chosen to destroy the entire future of mankind based on original sin alone, not to mention their lack of contrition afterwards. At the very least, He could have banished them from the Garden and left them to their own demise, with total indifference as to their fate. Yes, God could have done these things, but He didn't. Instead, He gave them a promise of a savior and the gift of a mother (see Gen 3:15). Moreover, He showed them how to receive His mercy, and it is as easy as A-B-C.

Thanks to Fr. George Kosicki, that's our handy shorthand for explaining the *message of Divine Mercy*:

> *Ask* for God's mercy.
> *Be* merciful to each other.
> *Completely* trust in God's mercy.

Knowing and living this message is a critical part of God's plan for mankind and his salvation. Pope Benedict XVI underscored its importance by saying the message of Divine Mercy is the "nucleus of the Gospel."[7] So if we reject Divine Mercy, in essence, we reject the Gospel. That was the real issue with Adam and Eve, not only that they fell into sin, but they didn't know their ABCs!

But isn't Divine Mercy simply a devotion, and aren't devotions optional in the Catholic Church? Yes, in one sense, Divine Mercy is a devotion given by Jesus to St. Faustina (which we will describe in detail in Chapters Three and Four), but it is not *simply* a devotion. Divine Mercy is both a **message** *and* a **devotion**. And while devotions are technically optional in the Catholic Church (for example, you don't necessarily have to pray the St. Michael chaplet to get to Heaven, although it is highly recommended), a *message* revealed by God, such as the message of Divine Mercy in Sacred Scripture, is not optional.

Now let's look at the ABCs of mercy in particular, to explore how the Gospels tell us they are an integral part of our spiritual life.

Ask for God's Mercy: We know we must do this in order to have eternal life with God forever in Heaven. The Bible tells us that unless we repent and ask for forgiveness, we cannot enter the Kingdom of God (see Lk 13:3, 5; Mt 18:3-4).

Be Merciful to Others: We know we must also do this in order to have eternal life. Examples such as Matthew 25:31-46 (to be explained in the next section) and other passages give us a stern warning from Jesus Himself about the necessity of being merciful. Showing mercy is so necessary, in fact, that our very salvation depends on it.

Completely Trust in God's Mercy: We cannot get to Heaven without grace, and Jesus told St. Faustina that all grace is received through one vessel only, and that vessel is *trust* (we will also explain this in more detail shortly).

Thus it is clear that living the *message* of Divine Mercy is not optional — it is needed to help us grow in the necessary virtues that will prepare us for eternal life. The message of Divine Mercy is that God loves us, all of us, no matter how great our sins. He wants us to recognize that His mercy is greater than our sins so that we will call upon Him with trust, receive His mercy, and let it flow through us to others. God wants us to turn to Him with trust and repentance while we are still living in the time of mercy, before He comes as the Just Judge.

A Deeper Look at the ABCs

These elements of the message of Divine Mercy may appear simple, but they are most profound. Thus, it is warranted to go into more detail on each one, mainly because we need to live each one if we hope to get to Heaven.

Ask for God's Mercy

God wants us to approach Him, to repent of our sins, and to ask Him to pour His mercy out upon us and upon the whole world. He tells us through the Apostle of Divine Mercy, St. Faustina, "**I cannot punish even the greatest sinner if he makes an appeal to My compassion, but on the contrary, I justify him in My unfathomable and inscrutable mercy**" (*Diary*, 1146). Jesus adds, "**I do not want to punish aching mankind, but I desire to heal it, pressing it to My Merciful Heart** (*Diary*, 1588).

The Lord makes it clear where this healing begins: in the confessional, through the Sacrament of Reconciliation. Confession is the best way to ask for God's mercy! Jesus tells St. Faustina:

> **Tell souls where they are to look for solace, that is, in the Tribunal of Mercy** [the Sacrament of Reconciliation]. **There the greatest miracles take place ... . [It] suffices to come with faith to the feet of My representative** [a priest] **and to reveal to him one's misery, and the miracle of Divine Mercy will be fully demonstrated. Were a soul like a decaying corpse so that from a human standpoint there would be no** [hope of] **restoration and everything would already be lost, it is not so with God. The miracle of Divine Mercy restores that soul in full** (*Diary*, 1448).

Moreover, we need not fear to ask for His mercy:

> **When you approach the confessional, know this, that I Myself am waiting there for you. I am only hidden by the priest, but I Myself act in your soul. Here the misery of the soul meets the God of mercy** (*Diary*, 1602).

After all, as the Gospels reveal, Jesus did not come to congratulate those who lead holy lives. Rather, He came for sinners. He tells us through St. Faustina, "**The greater the**

sinner, the greater the right he has to My mercy" (*Diary*, 723). So we who are sinners, we who seek forgiveness and healing, have but one thing to do: *Ask for it.*

Be Merciful to Others

God wants us to receive His mercy and, in turn, be merciful to others through our actions, words, and prayers. He wants us to extend love and forgiveness to others just as He extends love and forgiveness to us. In fact, this isn't just something He "wants"; rather, it is something He *demands*. Mercy is love that seeks to relieve the misery of others. It is an active love poured out upon others to heal, to comfort, to console, and to forgive. Mercy is the love that God offers to us, and, indeed, it is the love He demands from us for each other: "A new commandment I give to you, that you love one another; even as I have loved you, that you also love one another" (Jn 13:34, RSVCE). "Be merciful, even as your Father is merciful" (Lk 6:36, RSVCE).

As we said, the Scriptures remind us that even the strongest faith is of no use without works of love. The measure we use for others is the measure God will use for us (see Lk 6:38), for He will indeed "forgive us our debts, as we also have forgiven our debtors" (Mt 6:12, RSVCE). The parables of the Good Samaritan, the Rich Man and Lazarus, the Return of the Prodigal Son, and the Unforgiving Servant all demonstrate the essential truth that, having received mercy, we have the obligation to share it.

As the parable of the Sheep and the Goats in Matthew 25 tells us, we will be judged on the basis of our merciful actions toward others (see Mt 25:31-46). This parable gives us a picture of what it will be like at the end of time, when the king (Jesus) will judge the world, dividing the righteous from the unrighteous, just as "a shepherd separates the sheep from the goats" (25:32, NABRE).

On His right, He will place the sheep and He will say to them, "Come, you who are blessed by my Father. Inherit the kingdom prepared for you from the foundation of the world. For I was hungry and you gave me food, I was thirsty and you gave me drink, a stranger and you welcomed me, naked and you clothed me, ill and you cared for me, in prison and you visited me" (Mt 25:34-36, NABRE). And the sheep will ask, "Lord, when did we see you hungry and feed you, or thirsty and give you drink? When did we see you a stranger and welcome you, or naked and clothe you? When did we see you ill or in prison, and visit you?" (25:37-39). And He will reply, "Amen, I say to you, whatever you did for one of these least brothers of mine, you did for me" (25:40).

Sorry, goats. We know that Jesus will not say to you, "That's okay, I know you were too busy." Rather, He will place you on His left and say to you, "Depart from me, you accursed, into the eternal fire prepared for the devil and his angels. For I was hungry and you gave me no food, I was thirsty and you gave me no drink, a stranger and you gave me no welcome, naked and you gave me no clothing, ill and in prison, and you did not care for me" (Mt. 25:41-43, NABRE). And you will ask, "Lord, when did we see you hungry or thirsty or a stranger or naked or ill or in prison, and not minister to your needs?" (25:44). And He will reply, "Amen, I say to you, what you did not do for one of these least ones, you did not do for me" (25:45).

In other words, to get to Heaven we have to be merciful to each other. There's no other choice here.

Our Lord speaks to us through St. Faustina about the importance of deeds of mercy. He says:

I demand from you deeds of mercy, which are to arise out of love for Me. You are to show mercy to your neighbors always and everywhere. You must not shrink from this or try to excuse or absolve yourself from it. I am giving you three ways of exercising mercy

> toward your neighbor: the first — by deed,
> the second — by word, the third — by prayer.
> In these three degrees is contained the fullness
> of mercy, and it is an unquestionable proof
> of love for Me. ... [E]ven the strongest faith
> is of no avail without works (*Diary*, 742). ...
> If a soul does not exercise mercy somehow or
> other, it will not obtain My mercy on the day
> of judgment (*Diary*, 1317).

So, if you can't do something nice for somebody because you can't even be in the same room with them, you can certainly say something nice about them. You may rebut, "No Father, I can't even say something nice about Aunt Emma." Well, okay, but then you can at least *pray* for Aunt Emma. Whether in word, deed, or prayer, Christ says we must be merciful to each other, or we will not enter the kingdom of God.

The important thing to remember about mercy is that it requires you to put love into action. John Paul II stated that mercy is "love's second name."[8] Saint Faustina put it this way: "God's love is the flower, mercy is the fruit" (*Diary*, 949). So it is important that I share with you some great ways to put love into action through what the Church calls the Corporal and Spiritual Works of Mercy:

Corporal Works of Mercy

1. Feed the hungry
2. Give drink to the thirsty
3. Clothe the naked
4. Shelter the homeless
5. Comfort the prisoners
6. Visit the sick
7. Bury the dead

Spiritual Works of Mercy

1. Teach the ignorant
2. Pray for the living and the dead
3. Correct sinners
4. Counsel those in doubt
5. Console the sorrowful
6. Bear wrongs patiently
7. Forgive wrongs willingly

Completely Trust in Jesus

As I mentioned, Jesus told St. Faustina that humanity would not have peace until it turns with trust to His mercy (see *Diary*, 300). The need for trust is the very essence of the message of Divine Mercy and is the central theme throughout the entire Bible and the *Diary* of St. Faustina. It entails surrendering our will to God, dedicating our lives to Him, and entrusting ourselves to His care in good times and in bad. It entails entering into an authentic love with the One who loves us, even when we sin. In turn, we must trust that He wants what's best for us. We show that trust by obeying His commandments.

But what if we struggle to trust? Jesus understands our doubts. That's why He tells St. Faustina to **"fight for the salvation of souls, exhorting them to trust in My mercy, as that is your task in this life and in the life to come"** (*Diary*, 1452). To help us do this, He has given us a recourse in St. Faustina. In fact, He orders her to assist us. Today, in this age of doubt, we can turn to her in prayer and ask her to help us to trust more — to trust in God and to trust that, through God's grace, we are capable of sanctity. The more we trust, the larger the vessel we possess to receive the graces God wishes to give us.

Our Lord tells St. Faustina:

> **I have opened My Heart as a living fountain of mercy. Let all souls draw life from it. Let them approach this sea of mercy with great trust** (*Diary*, 1520). **... On the cross, the fountain of My mercy was opened wide by the lance for all souls — no one have I excluded!** (*Diary*, 1182). **... I delight particularly in a soul which has placed its trust in My goodness** (*Diary*, 1541). **... The graces of My mercy are drawn by means of one vessel only, and that**

is — trust. The more a soul trusts, the more it will receive (*Diary*, 1578).

Trust is a living faith. By trusting, we agree to not dwell on the past or to fear the future, but rather entrust our entire existence to the Providence of God. As one seventh grader put it, "Jesus, I trust in You" means that you know God is God, and you are not!

Jesus indicates that trusting in Him is the key to having our prayers answered: **"Most dear to Me is the soul that strongly believes in My goodness and has complete trust in Me. I heap My confidence upon it and give it all it asks"** (*Diary*, 453). He wants us to know that the graces of His mercy can only be received if we trust.

Salvation History is the History of Divine Mercy

Now let me give you the essence of everything you have read thus far. The best way to do that is to summarize the entire Bible in three points:

1. The Bible is a love story: It starts with a wedding and ends with a wedding.

The Bible starts with the marital covenant of Adam and Eve, and believe it or not, ends with a nuptial union. Contrary to popular belief, the last book of the Bible, the Book of Revelation, is not about the Antichrist or the rapture. It doesn't even mention the word "Antichrist" (although the "beast" is mentioned in Chapter 13), and the most popular form of belief in the rapture is a false doctrine created by John Darby in 1830. These words are not found in the Book of Revelation, but what *is* reflected on each page is the Mass. (For a great commentary on how the Book of Revelation is tied to the Catholic Mass, please read Dr. Scott Hahn's *The Lamb's Supper*.) As discussed previously, the Mass is best described as the Wedding Feast of the Lamb.

The Bible is a love story about God (the Groom) who is passionately trying to woo his unfaithful Bride, Israel (now the Church), back to Himself by regaining its trust in Him. The reason it's so hard for us to trust God is that after the fall, we became scared, skittish creatures. We're afraid; we're skeptical; we're broken.

He gave us Mary as a creature, one of our own as an intercessor, so that we would not fear to approach Him. God is a frightful being to many people, transcendent and out of our reach. But Mary helps bridge the gap. She's a creature like us, so even if we don't trust Him completely yet, He knows that we can trust the loving care of a benevolent mother. If we do, that mother will gently lead us back to God, which has been His plan ever since the fall of mankind.

Many people believe all you need to get to Heaven is faith, but according to Scripture, that is not entirely true. Abraham had faith in God, but if he didn't *trust* Him, he wouldn't have been willing to sacrifice Isaac. I can have faith in God, but if He asked me to sacrifice my son, I could say *no* because I don't have trust in Him. When Abraham was willing to obey the Lord's command to sacrifice Isaac (see Gen 22:1-18), it was not a matter of obedience only. It was a matter of trust.

God had promised Abraham that through his son Isaac, He would make his descendants as numerous as the stars in the sky (see Gen 15:15). Abraham could reasonably have asked, "Now you're asking me to kill him? How in the world, Lord, are you going to make my nation and my progeny as vast as the stars or the sands on the shore if you're telling me to kill this boy through which it's going to happen?"

Still, Abraham was willing to do it. And his willingness wasn't just a matter of blind obedience — it came from trust. You can imagine him praying, "Lord, I don't know how you're going to do it, but you're going to do it somehow, even if you have to raise this little child from the dead. I will obey you *because* I trust in you."

2. The two greatest commandments can be summarized into one: Do the will of God.

Jesus said the greatest commandments are to love God and love your neighbor as yourself (see Mt 22:36-40). According to the saints, these two can be rolled up into one: That one commandment is "Do the will of God." If you live the ABCs of mercy, you're loving God and loving your neighbor — you are doing His will. You are to **ask** for God's mercy. That's His will. You are to **be** merciful to each other. That's His will. You are to **completely** love and trust Him. That's His will.

3. Live the ABCs and get to Heaven.

Years ago I remember hearing about the bestselling book *All I Really Need to Know I Learned in Kindergarten.*[9] The author, Robert Fulghum, had written some simple rules for life. But in reality, everything you need to know is contained in the ABCs of Divine Mercy. The key to eternal life is loving God and our neighbor, trusting Him, and asking for forgiveness when we fail in those areas. Basically, it is living the ABCs of mercy. If you haven't read the Bible cover to cover, it's summarized in those ABCs. That's it.

That's why we must listen to the words of Jesus, who told St. Faustina that Divine Mercy is mankind's **"last hope of salvation"** (*Diary*, 965, 998). It truly is a matter of life and death. Jesus said to Faustina, **"He who refuses to pass through the door of My mercy must pass through the door of My justice"** (*Diary*, 1146). I don't know about you, but I'm not making it through the doors of God's justice. I need to go through the doors of His mercy! All of us do. That is why John Paul II said, "There is nothing that man needs more than Divine Mercy."[10] And he consecrated the world to Divine Mercy in 2002.

~ CHAPTER TWO ~

Saint Faustina:
Her Life and Spirituality

Many Prophets and Saints

As we learned in Chapter One, since the time of Adam and Eve, God has been trying to give us the message of Divine Mercy: a realization that we must ask for His mercy, we must be merciful to each other, and we must trust in His mercy.

We discussed how embracing the message of Divine Mercy is not optional, because it is the "nucleus" of the Gospel, and living the message is necessary in order to get to Heaven. That is why God has revealed this message to mankind. Divine Mercy is our spiritual blueprint from which we overcome concupiscence — that is, the inner corruption and disorder that we now battle in our fallen human nature. It is the way to live a virtuous life.

Remember, one of the ways to understand mercy is to know that it is the particular mode of love such that when it encounters suffering, it takes action to do something about it. Well, it didn't take God long to "do something" about the suffering that came to man as a result of the fall. In fact, He acted immediately by giving us the promise of a Savior and the gift of a mother (see Gen 3:15). Jesus and Mary are the answer to everything. They are the most incredible gifts that a loving Father could ever give His children — especially *wayward* children. That is true mercy.

But God didn't stop with Jesus and Mary. Throughout human history, as we discussed, God has been trying to call His Bride (us, the Church) back to Himself despite our unfaithfulness and our innate fear of Him. All He wants from us is trust, to trust in His goodness and mercy. To call us, God has been raising up great prophets and saints throughout the centuries to bring us this message of hope. He has never stopped seeking out His Bride by showing her how much He desires to be in union with her.

Our Lord's effort to foster a loving trust from His creatures so they will accept His love and choose to be united with Him has been the theme of salvation history. It has played out in countless ways: from the gift of His Son and the mother of His Son; from the gift of the Church and the Sacraments of the Church; from the words of the prophets and the saints and the example of these prophets and saints. These gifts have brought us a deeper understanding of this loving God of ours, our *Abba*, our Father. God has revealed Himself to us because He is fully aware that in our human nature, we cannot love what we do not know. Thus, He wants us to know Him so we can love Him more, and ultimately trust Him more.

The problem, however, is that sin has infected us. Our human nature is now "broken" and causes us to ignore, doubt, or even deny the mercy of God. Since we were created, we keep falling away, only to have God call us back to Him, only to fall away again. We're a stubborn and "stiff-necked people" (Ex 32:9, RSVCE) who put our trust in ourselves rather than in our Creator. This is why pride is the root of all sin, the *king* of all sin. To be prideful is to put ourselves on the throne, rather than place God, the true King, on the throne of our lives.

A Special Devotion Given to a Special Saint

Despite all that, God has never ceased His efforts to love us and call us to Himself. Moreover, His efforts reached a new level in the beginning of the 20th century. After thousands of years and after sending thousands of saints and prophets to reveal His love for us, only to be met with outright rejection in such ways as the heresy of Jansenism, God in essence said, "That's it — I am done here." Of course, He never used those exact words, and God is never "done" with us; His love for us never ceases. But in essence that is what He meant when He raised up yet another great saint named Helena Kowalska (whom we know today as St.

Maria Faustina Kowalska of the Blessed Sacrament) and told her, **"You will prepare the world for My final coming"** (*Diary*, 429).

Think about the significance of this fact: After taking so much effort to reveal Himself to mankind through so many messengers, the Lord gives St. Faustina this incredible responsibility. Christ gives this role to an "insignificant" nun whom John Paul II described as a poor girl, a girl from nowhere.[11] So who is this person to whom God would give one of the most monumental tasks in all of human history?

Remember, the message of Divine Mercy (that God loves us and wants to shower His mercy upon us as long as we ask for mercy, show mercy to others, and trust in His mercy) is nothing new. That message has been with us since the beginning. However, living this message of mercy has not been easy. We have rejected it since the beginning of time, showing we are in need of much grace if we are to practice it in our daily lives. Despite the difficulties, however, this has to be our goal.

To help us accomplish this task, Jesus gave Faustina five incredible new channels of grace to help us live the message of Divine Mercy in a deeper way. And what do we collectively call those five new channels of grace? We call them the *devotion* to Divine Mercy. We can remember another handy acronym when referring to the devotion to Divine Mercy: FINCH.

F = The **Feast** of Divine Mercy
I =   The **Image** of Divine Mercy
N = The **Novena** of Divine Mercy
C = The **Chaplet** of Divine Mercy
H = The **Hour** of Divine Mercy

We mentioned in Chapter One that devotions in the Catholic Church are technically optional, and you don't necessarily need them to get to Heaven. So then why bother? Because the *devotion* to Divine Mercy can help you live the *message* of Divine Mercy better. Think of the message of Divine Mercy (the ABCs) as what matters most; it's how you actually live your life. It is the basis on which you will be judged by God at your particular judgment. It is like an athlete being judged on how he performs in the game — the way you play the game is what really matters.

However, no athlete plays in the game without having first practiced. Think of the devotion to Divine Mercy (FINCH) as the practice — the practice that improves how you perform in the game of life. The practice of the devotion to Divine Mercy will ultimately help you become stronger in how you live the ABCs of mercy, which will get you to Heaven. The practice of any true devotion helps us to live a more Christlike life, one of love and virtue; but this devotion is of particular importance.

That being said, there is another important point to ponder. Unlike other devotions, the devotion to Divine Mercy is not just a devotion to another saint, like St. Thérèse or St. Anthony (as great as they are). No, the devotion to Divine Mercy is a devotion to God, and devotion to God is not optional. It is something integral to our spiritual life.

Paradoxically, we can also describe the devotion to Divine Mercy in a unique way in that it is not just about our devotion to God, but about God's devotion to us! In the Image of Divine Mercy, which we will describe in detail, we see Jesus' left foot stepping forward toward us. He is coming out of the darkness to us, to invite us to accept Him. This reveals the true devotion of the Creator to His creatures (much more on this to come).

Before we get into the details of these five new channels of grace known as the *devotion to Divine Mercy*, let's look a bit more at the life and spirituality of St. Faustina, the one Jesus trusted to bring these new channels of grace to the world.

Who Was St. Faustina?

Helena Kowalska (1905-1938) grew up as the third of 10 children in a small farmhouse on 12 acres of land in rural Poland. She was born on Aug. 25, 1905, to a peasant carpenter father and hardworking mother. Her family was quite poor but very religious, relying on a paltry sustenance provided from their tiny farm. As a small child, she was given the task of breaking up clods of dirt in the plowed fields, so she knew the value of hard work. She also knew the struggles that accompanied living in poverty. For example, she and her sisters had to share one dress between them, meaning that only one of them could attend Mass at a time. The fact that she could not attend church services regularly made Helena quite sad, and this showed that she had a natural love for God and her faith at a very early age.

She felt her first call to the religious life when she was only 7 years old, while spending time in Adoration of the Blessed Sacrament. Her mystical encounters continued. While she was still quite young and living at home, she already had a deep, spiritual understanding of the Mass.

In 1924, when she was 19, she and her sister Natalia went to a dance at a local park near her home in Poland. At the dance, she had a vision of a suffering Jesus, and He asked her, **"How long shall I put up with you and how long will you keep putting Me off?"** (*Diary*, 9). She saw Him as Christ crucified with all His wounds and blood-soaked scars. She took this to mean that she was to enter into religious life, so she immediately went to the nearby cathedral where she was told by Jesus to leave for Warsaw at once to join a convent there. Being obedient, she packed a small bag and took a train to Warsaw, 85 miles away, the very next morning. She did this without the permission of her parents, which was very rare for that time.

Not knowing anyone in Warsaw, she arrived a bit unsure of what course of action she should take. Thus, she trusted by surrendering completely to what she believed was Jesus' will for her. She entered the first Church she saw, the Parish of St. James the Apostle, and she attended Mass. There Jesus spoke to her internally and began to direct her as to what He wanted her to do. It was confirmed that she was to enter a convent and dedicate herself to Him through a vocation as a consecrated religious.

Helena then approached several convents in the Warsaw area, inquiring about entering their community, but she was turned down every time. Every convent essentially told her, "We do not accept maids here,"[12] referring to her poverty and her lack of education. The fact that she only had three winters of formal education and could barely read and write would later reveal how God can work through even the simplest of souls.

Helena's Entrance into Religious Life

After several weeks, the Mother Superior of the Sisters of Our Lady of Mercy gave her a chance. Helena didn't know anything about the convent or the religious community that she was joining; she only knew that Jesus had led her there. Some people would call this blind faith, but it was really an act of trust because she was listening in her heart to what Jesus was doing and where He was leading her. Because of this trust, she was rewarded with many graces that came from Christ revealing Himself to her.

The Mother Superior accepted her conditionally, provided she could pay for her religious habit, a common arrangement for newly entering members to religious life during that time. So in 1925, she worked as a housemaid to make money to pay for her religious garb and other basic expenses. Ironically, when she later went back to the convent, the Mother Superior didn't even remember her. By the grace of God, this problem was overcome, and she entered the Sisters of Our Lady of Mercy, receiving her habit in April

1926. There she took the religious name Maria Faustina of the Blessed Sacrament. Faustina means "fortunate" or "blessed one," which many believe is the feminine version of *Faustinus,* a martyr in the early centuries of the Church.

After she entered the community, she was assigned the duties of cook, gardener, and portress, which means she attended the door and received all visitors. She lived at different times in eight different convents in Poland and Lithuania, and she got to know the sisters everywhere she traveled. Some of these sisters questioned her and even mocked her because they thought she was not fully exerting herself in her daily duties, which were becoming very difficult for Faustina due to her declining health. Some believed she wasn't being honest about the severity of her sickness and even accused her of trying to be relieved of her work duties due to laziness; thus, numerous sisters seemed to dislike Faustina. Jesus encouraged her stay true to her vows, and over time some of the sisters came to accept her and even sought her counsel.

On February 22, 1931, when she was alone in her cell in Plock, Poland, Jesus came to her in person as the King of Divine Mercy, appearing as He is pictured in the Image of Divine Mercy. He was wearing the white garment with two rays — one red and one pale — emanating from His Heart. (We'll look at this Image more closely in Chapter Four.) Surprisingly, this was the only such apparition of Jesus that St. Faustina received in what is now Poland, as the rest were in Vilnius, which is now part of Lithuania, where she had been assigned by the superiors of her religious community.

Beneath her perceived dull existence, Faustina's deep inner life now overflowed with extraordinary mystical graces, divine revelations, and heavenly visitations. Christ began appearing frequently to her in visions. Sometimes He appeared as the King of Mercy, resplendent in light and majesty, and at other times as the tortured, crucified Christ.

The Diary

Jesus told Faustina to work with her confessor and to be truthful with him. He said if she hid anything from him, He would hide from her (see *Diary*, 269). So Faustina began to inform her confessor, Blessed Michael Sopocko, about these visions. He insisted that she have a complete psychiatric evaluation, which determined that her cognitive processes were completely normal. Father Sopocko began to believe Faustina and what she was telling him about the words Christ spoke to her, so he instructed her to write everything down in a diary. This written work, while very rough grammatically, was to become *Divine Mercy in My Soul*, more popularly known as the *Diary of Saint Maria Faustina Kowalska*.

In time, Fr. Sopocko not only believed Faustina, but he encouraged her to tell Jesus what was in her heart, and even to ask Him questions. Sopocko was an incredible priest; in fact, Jesus called him a priest after His own Heart (see *Diary*, 1256). What an incredible honor that must have been.

After St. Faustina began writing her diary, it was not surprising that she began to face temptations and attacks by the evil one. Demons would appear and decry her work and even profess their hatred of her because of the souls she was helping to save. Once, a demon played on the issue of humility and told her that her writing was an act of pride, which resulted in her decision to burn the diary and all its contents.

When he found out about this, Blessed Michael told Faustina to rewrite the diary as best she could. A problem arose, however, because as she was trying to reconstruct the original diary, she was continuing to have visions of Jesus. As a result, the current visions were mixed with the events she was recalling from her first diary, causing some chronological issues throughout the *Diary* we now have in publication. So, if you read the *Diary* today from cover to cover, it might be a bit confusing, because the events aren't always in sequential order. This also occurs in the Bible itself, so don't worry or be hesitant to read the *Diary*. The message of God's mercy runs through every page, no matter how you read it.

It is because of this *Diary* that St. Faustina is now known as the "Secretary and Apostle of Divine Mercy."

The Image

In 1934, Blessed Michael Sopocko introduced Sr. Faustina to the artist Eugene Kazimirowski, who actually lived in the priest's home. It was this artist who was commissioned to begin painting the Image of Divine Mercy as we know it today (specifically called the *Vilnius Image*). The three worked together to create this painting, based on Faustina's vision of Jesus in His appearances to her and following Christ's directive to paint the Image **"according to the pattern you see"** (*Diary*, 47). This wasn't an easy task, as she was not happy with the Image; in fact, she made Kazimirowski repaint it several times. Finally, Jesus told her in essence, "It's good enough." Here is what St. Faustina wrote about it:

> Once, when I was visiting the artist who was painting the image, and saw that it was not as beautiful as Jesus is, I felt very sad about it, but I hid this deep in my heart. When we had left the artist's house, Mother Superior [Irene] stayed in town to attend to some matters while I returned home alone. I went immediately to the chapel and wept a good deal. I said to the Lord, "Who will paint You as beautiful as You are?" Then I heard these words: **Not in the beauty of the color, nor of the brush lies the greatness of this image, but in My grace** (*Diary*, 313).

The Image of Divine Mercy has since become one of the most famous holy images in the world, along with the Shroud of Turin and the image of Our Lady of Guadalupe (we will discuss the Image in more detail in Chapter Four).

Finally, on Good Friday of 1935, Jesus told Faustina that He wanted this Image of Divine Mercy to be publicly honored. Father Sopocko followed this directive and also gave a sermon about Divine Mercy on the Sunday after Easter, which St. Faustina herself attended. This is evidence that the first modern Divine Mercy Sunday was celebrated in 1935, although it wasn't officially instituted by the Church until the year 2000.

Other Graces

At other times, Jesus gave St. Faustina the additional channels of grace included in what we call the devotion to Divine Mercy, such as the Chaplet of Divine Mercy (we will also discuss these other channels of grace in more detail in Chapter Four). He also gave her mystical experiences that she recorded in the *Diary*, such as visions of Heaven, hell, and Purgatory. Additionally, she was visited by Satan multiple times, appearing as himself and once disguised as an angel. Her holiness and humility was the antidote that frustrated Satan and any demon that tried to strike fear into her.

Saint Faustina was given many spiritual gifts, such as the ability to bilocate, and she even had the grace to read souls. Through these given graces, Jesus was preparing Faustina for future suffering that she was going to be asked to endure. He gave her a choice — as He does with us — to either accept this suffering or not. He said that if she did not freely accept it, it would be meaningless (see *Diary*, 190). Think about that in terms of our own suffering: If we have to suffer, we don't want it to be meaningless. Saint Faustina said "yes" to this suffering as she did to all things asked of her by Christ, so we have a great example in this pious nun. That is why, even though she received many consolations, she always remembered to place prayer as her first priority in order to persevere in such trials. Her spirituality could be summed up in an ancient Christian prayer that we know today as the "Jesus Prayer": "Lord Jesus Christ, Son of the Living God, have mercy on me, a poor sinner."

Saint Faustina suffered a great deal from tuberculosis as her lungs, tissue, brain, and bones were under agonizing attack. At Christ's request, she offered these sufferings in union with Him on the Cross to atone for the sins of others. This was a tremendous grace, one that allowed her to join in mystical union with Him, to put her sufferings to divine use, and to transform them into a daily oblation for the salvation of souls.

So here's the question for us: Are we also being asked by Jesus to share in a part of His Cross? In some way, all of us are. Some of our sufferings may be just "slivers" of the Cross, while others may be entire "beams." And although it may not seem this way sometimes, He will never give us more than we can handle with His grace. Yes, He does ask certain souls to suffer more; so if you have a lot of suffering, it may be because you are called by Christ to share in a larger portion of His Cross. While this may seem discouraging, it is in fact an incredible gift.

God's Plan

God's plan was that the suffering and challenges Faustina would endure would perfect her in trust and obedience in preparation for her mission. She received multiple internal (invisible) stigmatas, which we call *spiritual stigmatas*. She also suffered the pains and symptoms of abortion three times, losing consciousness due to the pain. She wrote that this was to offer reparation to God for the souls murdered in the wombs of their mothers (see *Diary*, 1276).

In the midst of her suffering, however, God did give Faustina additional consolations. She was one of only three people (that we know of) ever to behold a Seraphim angel. That puts her in company with the prophet Isaiah, who was visited by a Seraphim angel who touched his lip with a burning coal (see Is 6:6-7), and with St. Francis, who was visited by a Seraphim before receiving his stigmata. In only the third known instance of such a visitation, a Seraphim angel brought Faustina Holy Communion when she was too sick to attend Mass.

Interestingly, St. Faustina had a remarkable vision of her own canonization as well as visions of Divine Mercy Sunday celebrations in her chapel and in Rome (see *Diary*, 1044-1048). She described how she saw crowds in both her chapel and in the chapel in Rome simultaneously. In a fascinating account of her future canonization, she described St. Peter standing between the altar and the Holy Father, and how he spoke to the Holy Father although she could not hear his words. Regarding this vision, it's interesting to note that immediately after her actual canonization in 2000, Pope John Paul II announced that Divine Mercy Sunday was going to be placed on the universal calendar as an official feast in the Church. This proclamation was a surprise to many, for it had not been placed on the agenda for the day's events. It seems the pope was not planning to make the announcement, but perhaps St. Peter told him to do it? It's incredible to think about.

During Faustina's life, word started to spread regarding her visions, and under Popes Pius XI and Pius XII, imprimaturs were given for her writings as bishops began to support Divine Mercy and make it an approved devotion. On her sickbed, she predicted that a terrible war would break out and that it would be the deadliest conflict in human history. This war, World War II, began in Poland less than one year after she died.[13] Knowing that the war was coming, Jesus told her to pray for her country. Faustina also asked the nuns of her congregation to pray for Poland, leaving us an example that we should pray for our own nation as well.

After much suffering and supernatural efforts to do everything Jesus asked of her, St. Faustina finally succumbed to tuberculosis on Oct. 5, 1938. Today, we celebrate that date as her feast day, which has been added the Church's Universal Calendar and confirms the importance of her work in spreading Divine Mercy.

The Role of the Marian Fathers

One of the "main characters" in the spread of this message and devotion was Marian priest Fr. Joseph Jarzebowski, MIC, who personally knew Blessed Michael Sopocko. In 1941, hardly three years after the death of St. Faustina, he brought the Divine Mercy devotion to the United States from Poland — with the help of the grace of God.

Father Jarzebowski had at first been skeptical about the great graces reported by those who entrusted themselves to the Divine Mercy. But, in the spring of 1940, he knew that he had to flee Poland to escape the dangers of the war. He vowed that if he were able to safely reach his fellow Marians in America, he would spend the rest of his life spreading the Divine Mercy message and devotion.

Before his departure, Blessed Michael gave Fr. Jarzebowski materials on Divine Mercy that he had prepared. Carrying these materials and facing seemingly insurmountable obstacles, Fr. Jarzebowski set out on his journey. He couldn't travel west because of Nazi occupation, so he had to go east — and he had to do it with expired papers and visas. In fact, the materials he carried were considered contraband and would have been grounds for capture and perhaps even execution. Trusting in Divine Providence, he miraculously made it past several checkpoints without the materials ever being discovered.

After an extraordinary journey from Poland into Lithuania, then across Russia and Siberia to Vladivostok, and from there to Japan, he arrived on American soil a year later. True to his vow, he immediately began distributing information about the Divine Mercy message and devotion with the help of the Felician Sisters in Michigan and Connecticut. His Marian confreres soon became intensely involved as well.

In 1944, after several years of this activity, Fr. Walter Pelczynski, MIC (the first director of the Association of Marian Helpers), established the "Mercy of God Apostolate" on Eden Hill in Stockbridge, Massachusetts, now home of the National Shrine of The Divine Mercy. On these grounds is the Marian Helpers Center, where the Marian Fathers operate a modern religious publishing house that has become the international center for this Divine Mercy work. Since this ministry began here, this important message has never stopped spreading. Even soldiers going overseas during World War II helped to spread the message, including as far away as the Philippines. By 1953, some 25 million pieces of Divine Mercy literature had been distributed around the world.

Approved, then Banned, then Approved

In 1959, not long after the Divine Mercy devotion began quickly spreading across the globe, a "bombshell" was dropped that seriously impacted its promotion. Rome banned access to the Divine Mercy Images and to all the writings about Divine Mercy. Saint Faustina had foretold this in her *Diary* (see entry 378). The ban stemmed from a poor translation of the *Diary* from Polish into Italian. The translation contained many confusing statements, such as one — from *Diary* entry 1273, **"I am Love and Mercy itself"** — which when translated into Italian made it seem as if St. Faustina was saying this about herself.[14]

So the Church in her wisdom banned the writings until such time as they could be clarified. Then, praise God, in 1978, a short time before John Paul II became pope, the ban was lifted. Once inaugurated, Pope John Paul II spearheaded a new effort to study Faustina's writings and bring this treasure chest of graces to the Catholic faithful. Shortly after this, our very own Fr. Seraphim Michalenko, MIC, smuggled pictures of the *Diary* passages from communist Poland into the United States, which were then translated into English and made available on a much wider scale to the American Church.

The exclusive mission of St. Faustina's life was this: Trust in the mercy of God and plead mercy for the whole world. We, too, are called to do this. Her mission is our mission. The spirituality of St. Faustina was entirely about trust and mercy. She totally surrendered to God's will, as was seen in the fact that she accepted tasks from Jesus that she couldn't possibly do on her own, without the assistance of His grace. For instance, He asked her to paint, but she wasn't an artist. He asked her to spread the Divine Mercy devotion around the world, but she had no money. He asked her to have Divine Mercy Sunday celebrated in the universal Church, but she had no influence in the Church. You get the point.

Jesus did give her some help in Fr. Sopocko, but He held her accountable for the souls that would not be saved if she didn't do all of these seemingly impossible tasks. Why would Jesus do that? Our Lord was testing her to see how much she would trust in Him, and it was through trust that St. Faustina knew Jesus was with her the whole way.

Back in the United States, as Fr. Seraphim began to study St. Faustina's writings, the cause for her beatification became a topic for discussion. In a relatively short period (in Church terms), she was beatified on the basis of a miracle experienced by Maureen Digan, a very good friend of our Marian community here at the National Shrine of The Divine Mercy. Maureen was healed of lymphedema, a disease for which there is no cure. Later, St. Faustina's canonization was approved based on the miraculous cure of Fr. Ron Pytel from an incurable heart condition.

Now that Faustina has become a saint, we continue to pray for her to become the fifth female Doctor of the Church. Her writings about Divine Mercy with their encouraging message of trust in Jesus are the means by which she is preparing the world for His final coming. Awareness of Divine Mercy has certainly spread; as we mentioned, Fr. Seraphim has called Divine Mercy "the greatest grass roots movement in the history of the Catholic Church." And one of the main promulgators of Divine Mercy, John Paul II, essentially said that "it was precisely to this poor girl, a girl from nowhere, that God entrusted the mission of announcing to the whole world the most important message of the twentieth century."[15] Isn't this amazing?

The School of Trust

We finished the last chapter mentioning that this message of trust is the same message found in the Bible. In that chapter we stated the big problem with Adam and Eve wasn't only the fact that they sinned, it was that they didn't trust and believe what God told them. The serpent gave them a distorted image of God, making them believe that He was someone they should fear. Satan is all about distrust; he tells us we can only trust ourselves, which brings slavery, not freedom. We become slaves of the things that we think will fulfill us — our sexuality, our appetites, our weak wills. This only brings unhappiness and fear as those things will fail us.

I once heard it said that fear was cited as one of the main reasons why people don't go to church. They're afraid of the God who sets the rules. So, trusting God is the key to overcoming such fear. In fact, "Be not afraid" were the first words spoken by John Paul II when he became pope, and these same words are stated 365 times in the Bible.

Let's look at what Fr. Michael Gaitley, MIC has to say about fear and what he calls the "school of trust" found in the Bible:

When Adam and Eve hear God walking in the garden, rather than run to Him, they run away. Rather than acknowledge their sin, confess it and jump into the embrace of God's love, they hide. Rather than trust in our infinitely good and merciful God, they're afraid of Him.

Man, tempted by the devil, let his trust in his Creator die in his heart and, abusing his freedom, disobeyed God's command. This is what man's first sin consisted of. All subsequent sin would be disobedience toward God and lack of trust in his goodness (*Catechism*, 397).

Now notice that the key word here is "trust." The first sin begins with a lack of trust. It says man let his trust in his Creator die in his heart. And this root of sin applies not only to the first sin but as the *Catechism* says, "to all subsequent sin." Indeed, every one of our sins involves lack of trust in God's goodness. The *Catechism* goes on to include this lack of trust as one of the "tragic consequences" of sin. Getting even more specific, it says that "Adam and Eve become afraid of the God of whom they have conceived a distorted image …" And that right there, that part about the distorted image, explains a lot. And why does it explain a lot? Well, because that wound of having a distorted image of God has been passed on to us. I mean, every single one of us tends to fear God and lack trust in him. We tend to see Him as one who just wants to ruin our fun; one who's always ready to give us the divine smackdown; one who is jealous to hold onto His power over us.

But is that true? Is God some kind of spiteful and vindictive being who just likes to establish rules that no one can follow and then punish us for not following them? No, that's not who God is. Here's the reality: Our God is a father who burns with love for us and longs to make us happy. He shows infinite mercy toward us; not because He has to, but because He wants to. And if we really understood this in our hearts, then wouldn't it make sense to give him all of our trust? Yet, we don't. We need to get back to the kind of childlike innocence where we trust our Heavenly Father. Now unfortunately, we often don't have that kind of trust; we don't let ourselves fall into the loving arms of the Lord.

I know that trusting in the Lord is not easy. The distorted image of Him that we all have to one degree or another can be difficult to overcome. Yet, God works so hard to heal this wound in us. In fact, I'd say that all of salvation history can be summarized as God's great effort of trying to get us skittish, fearful creatures to give up our fear of Him and trust in His love and goodness.

In salvation history, in the story of Sacred Scripture, God is trying to teach us, trying to convince us to trust in Him so he can heal us and save us. And that's why I think the whole of the Bible can really be summarized as one long school of trust; one great effort on God's part to heal the distorted image of Him that each one of us has. And He wants to heal that wound in us so we'll begin to trust in Him again, so He can save us.[16]

Trust and Mary: Accepting the Help Offered to Us

Father Gaitley's idea of the "school of trust" reinforces what I said about trust being the key to our relationship with God. But you still might say, "Okay, Father, it's trust, but how do I apply it?" The best way to learn how to do this is to learn from someone's example. Who is the ultimate example of trust? Obviously, Mother Mary. We obtain trust through Mary because she is the new Eve. She is the opposite of the original Eve, because Eve was the "mother of distrust."

Mary did not fear; she gave her *fiat*, her "yes," when she could do nothing but place trust in what the Lord was telling her would happen. She is a gift that God gave to us as a mother, a creature like us, because He knew we would be afraid of Him after the fall in the Garden of Eden. And how do you ultimately show that you trust someone? You accept the help they offer you. Thus, the help God offers us through the gift of His mother is help that we should accept with trust.

When I was young and sometimes afraid that my father was disappointed in me because I had done something wrong, I ran to my mother. I did so because I was afraid that my dad would think I wasn't tough or that he wouldn't be happy with me. But my mom assured me that my dad wouldn't think that of me and that I had no reason to fear. This is what Mary can do for us. Mary is truly the new Eve, and she brings to us the new Adam (Jesus) on the new Tree of Life, the Cross. Thus, the old Adam, the old Eve, and the old Tree are all undone.

This is really what Marian consecration is all about: entrustment. It means trusting our guide, Mary, to bring us to Jesus. "To Jesus, through Mary" is the goal of this consecration. So ask her to help you to know God's will, because she always did it perfectly in her own life. There's nothing wrong with accepting other people's help — even Jesus did on His way to Calvary.

The Key to Happiness: Our Misery?

One of the most common questions I receive as a priest is, "How do I know God's will?" The Church teaches that obeying God's commandments and persevering in the daily duties of our state in life is living God's will. That said, you might be wondering, "There's got to be more to life than fighting traffic, being frustrated at work, getting home and having to make dinner, helping my children with their homework, trying to pay my bills while disagreeing with my spouse, and then getting up the next day and doing it all over again." In fact, this is exactly how we are sanctified: by faithfulness in our duties. No matter how difficult things become, remaining faithful to the people who depend on us brings many graces. Just ask St. Joseph, the worker.

Doing God's will and not our own will provides ultimate happiness because it brings the graces needed for salvation. The enemy of our salvation, sin, is nothing other than independence from God's will for our life. In other words, sin means not trusting. It is basically saying to God, "I'm going to do it my way, not Your way." Do you consult with God before you take a new job or move to a new city? Do you ask that God's will be done before you decide to make major changes in your life? If you don't, you may be acting contrary to God's will. And if you do that, you are making yourself more susceptible to sin, which ultimately cuts you off from God's grace.

When we cut ourselves off from God's grace, what are we? The answer is *miserable*. But don't despair, Jesus told us there is a huge opportunity here. Faustina said that the secret to happiness is to always be aware of one's own misery. *What?* Yes, because only then will we recognize our need for God's mercy; and many times that's why He allows our suffering. When we turn to Him in misery, we can then more fully receive His mercy.

Jesus further said to St. Faustina, **"Your misery does not hinder My mercy. My daughter, write that the greater the misery of a soul, the greater its right to My mercy;** [urge] **all souls to trust in the unfathomable abyss of My mercy, because I want to save them all"** (*Diary*, 1182).

Very few people realize that the key to happiness is an awareness of *both* our misery and God's mercy. If we do not accept the truth of our own limitations and our misery, we can't trust. If we only seek temporal happiness, thinking that will cover all of our spiritual miseries, we will never trust Jesus.

In his book *Stepping on the Serpent*, Fr. Thaddaeus Lancton, MIC, makes several great points about the para-doxical value of our misery.[17] He points out that many people came to Jesus because they recognized their misery and their inability to help themselves. Their suffering and misery brought them to their knees in a cry for mercy. Only then could Jesus help them. Father Lancton explains how acknowledging our need for God is the key to our salvation. Only when we bring our misery and helplessness to Jesus can He fully help us.

The Scriptures tell us that the only unforgivable sin is the sin against the Holy Spirit, the sin of final impenitence that happens when a soul says, "I don't need the mercy of God, I am fine. I am well respected, and I have health and money — I have all that I need." Don't fall into that trap; no earthly possessions or praises can provide true happiness. Jesus tells us that all we truly have is our misery. Happiness comes from His mercy.

Saint Faustina had this conversation with God:

I have given myself entirely to You; I have then nothing more that I can offer You. Jesus said to me, **My daughter, you have not offered Me that which is really yours.** I probed deeply into myself and found that I love God with all the faculties of my soul and, unable to see what it was that I had not yet given to the Lord, I asked, "Jesus, tell me what it is, and I will give it to You at once with a generous heart." Jesus said to me with kindness, **Daughter, give Me your misery, because it is your exclusive property.** At that moment, a ray of light illumined my soul, and I saw the whole abyss of my misery (*Diary*, 1318).

The Value of Surrender

This is the meaning of surrender. It's when you say, "Lord, I give it all to You. I can't do this anymore. I trust that somehow, some way, You will bring a greater good out of my suffering (more about this in Chapter Five). I don't see it, but I trust You will make it happen by being merciful to me, no matter how You determine to administer that mercy." Therefore, that doesn't mean that you will suddenly win the lottery to pay all your bills; in fact, God may extend periods where you have to go without. We're talking about surrendering to the will of God in your life, which isn't always the same as your will.

Father Lancton points out the temptation in thinking that mercy means being saved *from* the Cross, rather than being saved *through* the Cross. Even St. Peter made that huge mistake. Peter learned that lesson when he urged Jesus not to go to Jerusalem so He could avoid the Cross. Jesus rebuked him: "Get behind me, Satan!" (Mt 16:23, RSVCE). But ironically, even Satan plays a part in God's plan, because he is used to test us. God has tricked Satan, because He knows the devil will expose our poverty and our misery, which is the way we can be led to God's mercy. Satan wants us to believe we have nothing, and he will show us how weak and broken we are, which is exactly what God wants us to see! Talk about irony.

Remember, God wants to bring a greater good out of even the worst evil. When Satan exposes all of our downfalls and weaknesses, it doesn't have to lead us to despair, which is Satan's goal. It can actually be a good thing because it can bring us to the point where we say, "You're right, I have nothing — I need you Lord." This is what is needed to make us beg for mercy. As I remember reading one of the saints saying, "I will go before you Lord naked, with nothing but your mercy."

God often may seem silent to us, something even I admit to feeling from time to time. In our trials, it may seem like God is not there. But as Fr. Lancton emphasizes, the Cross is never God's last word. It is the Resurrection that is the last word. We just have to go through the Cross first in order to enter into the glory of the Resurrection. Saint Faustina wrote: "I do not ask, Lord, that You take me down from the cross, but I implore You to give me the strength to remain steadfast upon it" (*Diary*, 1484).

God may allow us to remain on the cross when our request to be removed from it is not in our best interest. It is true that many times we pray with the wrong motive (see Jas 4:3). That's why God doesn't always give us what we ask for or in the way we ask for it. One example could be praying for someone who's dying and asking God to let them live — living forever on this earth with all its suffering is not necessarily always a blessing.

If we ever want to be able to surrender completely and to accept our suffering with trust, we must first understand its value (this is the subject of the last chapter). Suffering can have two outcomes: It can lead us to distrust and bitterness, or it can lead us to trust, when we say, "Lord, now I need you more than ever." Blessed Sebastian Valfre (1629-1710) once said, "When it is all over you will not regret having suffered; rather you will regret having suffered so little, and suffered that little so badly."[18]

Although we shouldn't indiscriminately ask for more suffering, we shouldn't ignore suffering either. Again, Fr. Lancton makes some good points. He says we can and should complain to God. In fact, there are Psalms in the Bible called the *Psalms of Lament* (e.g., Ps 6, 86, 130), that can help us to express our true feelings to the Lord even when we are distressed and lacking trust. We can complain to a point, because it shows we believe God is listening. Don't be afraid to complain to Him, even if it is about other people testing our patience to the extreme. Even in this situation, God has the greater good in mind.

We can always see examples where Jesus uses worldly people for His glory; for instance, He allows people in our lives who try our patience because they give us the opportunity to grow in virtue. This frustration we have for such persons can raise our awareness of the need to pray for them, which, in turn, aids them in their own salvation. Only God could come up with a master plan like this. As mentioned, we will discuss this in more detail in Chapter Five.

Love is NOT Just an Emotion

Yes, loving those who frustrate us or cause us to suffer is very difficult, but we need to do so because Jesus says that "even sinners love those who love them" (Lk 6:32, RSVCE). So we are called to the most challenging kind of love, to love even those who hate and persecute us. How are we able to do that? Well, if love was just an emotion, we couldn't. Fortunately, love is not just an emotion, but rather an act of the will. I can *choose* to love you no matter what, for better or worse, for richer or poorer, just as spouses promise one another in their Catholic wedding vows.

I don't always feel the emotion of love when I'm angry with someone I care about. But I choose to love them even when I'm upset. If it were just about emotions, which go up and down like a roller coaster, no relationships would stand the test of time. In fact, that is exactly why so many marriages are ending in divorce today — the secular world has redefined love not based on the truth, but based on emotion. If we truly love someone, we will their good. Love is desiring the good of the other in all circumstances, even when they upset us.

A good example of this point is my sister, Pam. A few years ago her husband abandoned her after 24 years of marriage and two children because of an extramarital affair. He had been clandestinely seeing a woman for several years and one day announced to Pam, "I love you, but I'm not *in* love with you anymore." He immediately left and ended the marriage. To say my sister was devastated is an understatement — her whole world was gone in an instant.

If there was ever an example of someone having a good reason to be angry and vexed with another person, this was it. Although my ex brother-in-law was the one fully culpable, his "girlfriend" played a major part in the destruction of my sister's marriage. As Pam tried desperately to make sense of this senseless situation, she began to piece together more of the puzzle. She learned that the woman was a very troubled soul, one who had many wounds from the past such that her psychological state was extremely volatile.

She was so distressed, in fact, that one day after the divorce, my ex brother-in-law and she were in the car when they reached a railroad crossing. As the train was quickly approaching and they were waiting, they continued an argument that had been ensuing all morning. Reaching a boiling point, this woman suddenly and without explanation dashed out of the vehicle and proceeded to dive onto the tracks in front of the train just as it arrived. It literally cut her in half. She died instantly.

Now in an earthly sense, Pam had the right to dislike or even hate this woman. Instead, as I found out in a conversation with my sister years later, she had been earnestly praying for her every day since the moment of that tragedy. In utter amazement, I questioned Pam as to why she chose to do this, and she innocently said, "I pray for her all the time, even though I rarely feel like it. I do so because I know it is the right thing to do. She was a troubled person who obviously is in serious moral trouble, for both the adultery and for her own suicide. I realized that her soul may be in jeopardy, and there is never, ever a time we should want a soul to be lost, no matter who they are. I realized that if I forgave her as the one she hurt, God would forgive her too."

All I can say about those words is, "Wow!" Here I am the priest in the family, and my sister is teaching me what it is like to be a living example of Christ. If I can be half the true Christian that she is, I will consider myself a good man. I hope that one day I can reach the level of love and virtue that my sister has reached. God bless her.

Remember, the more valuable something is, the more we must pay to attain it. The most valuable thing in the world is the human soul, and all souls are purchased at a price. Jesus said to St. Faustina, **"[E]very conversion of a sinful soul demands sacrifice"** (*Diary*, 961). If souls are precious to us, no price is too high to pay. If not, then we will consider the cross that God gives us on their account as too heavy a price to pay.

The bottom line is that my sister had a choice: If she didn't care about that woman's soul, she could have just been glad the woman was out of her life — even that she was dead. But my sister made the choice to pray for her soul because she knows how precious a soul is. And no cross was too heavy to bear. So what this story tells us is that in return for something that causes us pain and suffering, which will eventually end, we can gain for ourselves and others eternal life that never ends.

Sometimes, however, it may seem that prayers for certain souls are a waste of time because they appear to be "too far gone" or seem to be unwilling to ever change. In fact, we can even feel that same way about ourselves. I have often heard people say, "Father, I don't go to church because it would be hypocritical of me to do so. You have no idea how bad a sinner I am." To them I always reply, "Really? You think your sins are greater than God's mercy? You might want to listen to what St. Faustina has to say about that!"

Are You Too Sinful to Receive God's Mercy?

Jesus told St. Faustina:

> **I desire trust from My creatures. Encourage souls to place great trust in My fathomless mercy. Let the weak, sinful soul have no fear to approach Me, for even if it had more sins than there are grains of sand in the world, all would be drowned in the unmeasurable depths of My mercy** (*Diary*, 1059).

Since God cannot change, even our sins cannot change His love for us. If you're feeling unloved, please don't. I can guarantee you that you are loved. In fact, you are loved by the most important being of all: God. If He didn't love you, you wouldn't be reading this sentence. The very fact that you are breathing and that you remain in existence is proof positive of God's love for you. God creates out of love and sustains out of love, and you were created and are now being sustained by this love. Even our sins cannot change that.

Surprisingly, healing our sin is not about doing more; rather, it is about receiving more. Even our brokenness will never stop the Father from loving us, so we might as well receive that love! As we said, God's love is like the sun — it never stops shining on us. I remember once being on an airplane during a rainy day; the clouds were thick and it was miserably cold, dark, and dreary outside. As we left the runway and ascended above the clouds, I was intrigued to notice that the sun was shining as bright as ever. It never stops shining. That is like God's love; even if we have a thick layer of sin and brokenness in our lives, His love is there for us. We need to clear away those clouds of distrust so that the rays of God's love — the rays of Divine Mercy — can shine brighter on us than ever before, and we can receive it to the full.

In Chapter One we talked about the works of mercy and why it is important to *do* these acts of love. But now I want to tie that into our current discussion of how to *receive* love. We always think that when we help the poor, it is the poor who are benefiting, and that is true in a physical sense. But in a spiritual sense, we are the ones who receive more than they, because it is the poor who open our hearts and give us the opportunity to be charitable in the first place. For that, we receive tons of grace. It is an awesome concept to think about.

Referring back to Fr. Lancton, he stresses that love is about giving *and* receiving. God says we are to give so much of ourselves that we become empty, so then we can receive and be filled by God. If we are filled with this world, God can't fill us with the world to come. Father Lancton explains that the Wedding Feast at Cana illustrates this point. Mary didn't expose the bride and groom and their family to the shame of running out of wine. Rather, she quietly brought the problem to Jesus, and in the same way Mary quietly brings our lack, our emptiness, and our brokenness to Jesus as well.

Satan screams, "Look at your lack! You are nothing but emptiness!" In the opposite way, Mary quietly takes that emptiness and fills it with Christ. Jesus desires to fill our emptiness in the same way that He filled the jars at Cana, with His divine wine. What wine is that? The Holy Spirit. We must keep in mind, however, that our trust and obedience are necessary for this to happen. As Jesus declared to St. Faustina, we need a vessel to receive all of this (like the jars at Cana), and that vessel is *trust*.

At Cana, Mary saw that the wine jars were empty and so she brought the problem to Jesus (see Jn 2:1-11). In a similar way she brings us in our emptiness to her Son. At the wedding, she didn't tell the Lord how to fix the problem; she waited with trust. Mary, who entrusted the empty jars to her Son to be filled, invites us to allow the emptiness of our spiritual "jars" — our hearts — to be filled as well. All we have to do is trust that He will do so.

We Need to Trust God, But Can He Trust Us?

Thus, we see that the key for us to be filled with God's mercy is to trust Him, but as unwarranted as it seems, God actually trusts us way more than we trust Him. Crazy, huh? An example would be our own family. God entrusts souls to us; in marriage, He entrusts your spouse to you as well as your children. That is a huge responsibility God has given you. That's why you need to trust Him by communicating with Him in prayer and asking Him to guide you to do His will in your life and in the lives of those you love. Deciding to get married means that you are building a bridge between the two of you and your misery, and between the two of you and God's mercy. The trials and tribulations of marriage and raising a family are opportunities for you to grow in virtue.

Building on this concept, the most important way that God trusts us is with His very self in the Eucharist. This is why the Devotion to Divine Mercy is not just about our devotion to God, it's also about God's devotion to us. So, can we not trust Him in return? Blessed Francis Xavier Seelos wrote, "None of the damned was ever lost because his sin was too great, but because his trust was too small."[19]

Again, this is what the life and spirituality of St. Faustina was all about: *trust* and *mercy*. Please take her message to heart — it is not an optional message, and you can't afford to ignore it. It is the key to Heaven. Jesus, I trust in You!

Now, let's look at these elements of the devotion to Divine Mercy that Jesus entrusted to St. Faustina to give to the world, starting with the greatest of them all, the Feast of Divine Mercy.

~ CHAPTER THREE ~

The Feast
of Divine Mercy

In the last chapter we summarized the amazing life and spirituality of St. Faustina. What makes both so truly remarkable is the fact that her life appeared so plain on the outside, and the simplicity of her character would lead many to assume that her spirituality was shallow on the inside. On the contrary, St. Faustina was filled with God's graces and reached the heights of sanctity, becoming a model for all Christians to follow. It shows that God can use anyone, even the simplest and most uneducated, to accomplish His will.

Saint Faustina had very limited formal education, yet she penned one of the great classics of Christian spirituality of our times, *Divine Mercy in My Soul,* which we introduced in the last chapter. We explained that Jesus, appearing to Faustina on multiple occasions and over a span of nearly eight years beginning in 1931, gave her five new channels of grace referred to as the *devotion to Divine Mercy.* This devotion has changed the world.

These new channels of grace were meant to be given to the world for the purpose of reawakening the ABCs of mercy, which we outlined earlier. While these ABCs — the *message of Divine Mercy* — form the basis of trust and mercy we need for our salvation, the elements of the devotion to Divine Mercy provide the graces we need to grow in trust and to be better disposed to receive God's mercy.

We'll discuss each of these five channels of grace in the coming chapters, but to quickly summarize, they are the **Feast** of Divine Mercy, the **Image** of Divine Mercy, the **Novena** of Chaplets, the **Chaplet** of Divine Mercy, and the **Hour** of Mercy (3 p.m.) — just remember the acronym **FINCH**. All of these came to St. Faustina directly from Jesus Himself, as He ached to immerse mankind in the fount of His mercy and shower upon us infinite graces from the abyss of His merciful Heart.

The Feast of Divine Mercy
(The Eighth Day)

Let's first discuss what may be the greatest of all the Divine Mercy graces: *The Feast of Divine Mercy*. What is this feast and when is it celebrated? The Feast of Divine Mercy, also known as *Divine Mercy Sunday*, is celebrated every year on the Second Sunday of Easter (the Sunday immediately following Easter Sunday).

Jesus made it clear, very clear in fact, that this feast had to be celebrated on this exact day, and the reasons for this are significant. As we will explain, it is the octave of the celebration of the feast of Easter, the day of Christ's Resurrection (*octave* means the eighth day after a feast). Referring to Easter Sunday as Day 1, and finishing the following Sunday, we refer to Divine Mercy Sunday as the "eighth day," or the "Octave of Easter." This day was given by Christ, through St. Faustina, as the ultimate day of grace. The reasoning for this goes back to the Jewish roots of Christianity.

Our Christian faith comes from the Jews, and as such we have adopted many of their traditions of religious worship and liturgical practices. One such example involves religious feasts and how they are celebrated. For important feasts of the Hebrew calendar, the Jewish people would celebrate a single feast for more than one day; in fact, they would celebrate one feast over eight consecutive days. Known as an *octave* in the Jewish faith, these important feasts were all festive days honoring and worshipping God, praising and thanking Him for the many blessings received from Him.

The reason Jewish festivals lasted for eight days was because the number eight is significant in Jewish tradition. To understand why, we need to back up a bit. According to the *Catholic Encyclopedia*, "It is actually the number seven, not eight, that plays the principal role in Jewish heortology [study of the history and meaning of sacred calendars] dominates the cycle of the year. Every seventh day is a

Sabbath; the seventh month is sacred; the seventh year is a sabbatical year."[20]

We know that the reason for this is Biblical: The number seven is the divine number of completion in the *natural* realm. God accomplished His work of creation in six days, but He completed this act of mercy by "resting" on the seventh day. Thus, seven is one of the most powerful numbers in Judaism, representing God's covenants with man as well as creation, good fortune, and blessing. The number seven symbolizes "the entirety of the natural world."[21]

Since eight comes after seven, it makes sense that the Jews believed this number has a spiritual significance that goes beyond the natural realm. They viewed eight as a number that symbolizes new beginnings; it is the number of completion in the *supernatural* realm. The eighth day was the day of circumcision (see Gen 21:4; Lev 12:3; Lk 1:59; Acts 7:8, etc.). The Feast of Tabernacles and the Feast of the Dedication of the Temple under Solomon are other examples of feasts that had celebrations on the octave day. An animal was acceptable as a sacrifice on the eighth day of its life. Many more examples abound. Therefore, the eighth (octave) day, believed by many not to have the same symbolic importance as the seventh day, may in fact be more important.

In the article "What is the Spiritual Significance of the Number Eight?" Eliezer Posner makes the following observations:

> In kabbalistic teachings, the number seven symbolizes perfection — perfection that is achievable via natural means — while eight symbolizes that which is beyond nature and its (inherently limited) perfection. Eight, on the other hand, is symbolic of an entity that is one step above the natural order, higher than nature and its limitations. That's why Chanukah is eight days long — the greatly out-

numbered Maccabees' resolve to battle the Greeks wasn't logical or natural. They drew on reservoirs of faith and courage that are not part of normative human nature. They therefore merited a miracle higher than nature — a miracle that lasted eight days — and to commemorate this, we light on Chanukah an eight-branched menorah.[22]

Because the Jews believed the number eight symbolized perfection and completion beyond our physical realm, it made perfect sense that Jesus demanded that the Feast of Divine Mercy be placed on the eighth day. It represents *eternity*, that which goes beyond the natural order and into the supernatural.

To better understand the significance of the eighth day, it might help us to look at two of our Catholic feasts: Christmas and Easter. In our tradition, we used to celebrate many of our feasts as octaves: We had the Octave of Pentecost, the Octave of Corpus Christi, and others. However, after recent reforms of the missal, we now celebrate only Christmas and Easter as octaves. So let's start with Christmas.

When does Christmas begin? The Christmas season technically begins on Christmas Day, or if you celebrate vespers, it begins on Christmas Eve. Basically, the Octave of Christmas begins on Christmas Day, Dec. 25, which is Day 1, and concludes the following week on Jan. 1, which is Day 8, or the eighth day. Why do we go to church every year on Jan. 1 no matter what day of the week it is? We go to celebrate the Solemnity of *Mary, the Mother of God*. And what you may not know is that Dec. 25, the celebration of the birth of our Lord, and Jan. 1, the Solemnity of Mary, the Mother of God, are celebrated as one feast called Christmas, and ending with ...)ctave Day of Christmas. This is because you cannot e the birth of Christ from Mary, His mother.

iat about Easter? As you know, Easter is the most t solemnity (meaning highest celebration) of our liturgical year. But you may not know that we also celebrate this feast over eight full days as well, which concludes with the Octave Day of Easter. We celebrate it beginning on Easter Sunday, Day 1, and ending on the following Sunday, which is *Divine Mercy Sunday*, or Day 8. The Roman Missal calls it the "Second Sunday of Easter" because it is the second Sunday in the Easter *season*, and this season actually extends all the way until *Pentecost* — 50 days after Easter.

The Octave of Easter

Divine Mercy Sunday is the last day of the Octave of Easter, the eighth day, which is the greatest day of the Octave, the *climax* of the whole feast. In a sense, Divine Mercy Sunday is the most important day of the most important feast! But why? Because of what the eighth day represents. It is a *completion* that goes beyond the completion of our natural world; it is a "new beginning" in the supernatural order. It is perfection beyond the perfection of the natural order and leads us to eternity.

Some may ask, "Why did God wait so long to bring us this greatest day of mercy?" In fact, He didn't. As you can find on our Marian website TheDivineMercy.org, this is explained in detail:

> The Feast of Mercy proclaims this same gospel message. It is not a new feast. According to St. Augustine, St. Gregory Nazianzen, and The Apostolic Constitutions, the early Church celebrated the Sunday after Easter, or Octave Day of Easter, as a great feast day (called in the West "Dominica in Albis" — the Sunday in White, which was a time of forgiveness of all sin and punishment). It was a rounding out of the eight days of Easter celebrations, and a day that St. Augustine is reported to have called "the compendium of the days of mercy." In other words, on this day the Church

gives thanks to God for His merciful love shining through all the great acts by which He won our salvation, especially the Cross and Resurrection of His Son. As Pope John Paul II said in his Regina Caeli address on Mercy Sunday, 1995, "the whole Octave of Easter is like a single day," and the Octave Sunday is meant to be a day of "thanksgiving for the goodness God has shown man in the whole Easter mystery."[23]

The problem was that nobody knew about this feast, so Jesus told St. Faustina that He wanted her to bring it to the world anew (See *Diary*, 341). The reason Christ emphasized this was because of the greatness of this day, as we read in the statements of John Paul II and St. Augustine above.

Think of how beautiful this is: Christ resurrected on Sunday, the day after the Jewish Sabbath (Saturday), the observed day of rest in honor of God's day of rest and the completion of creation. Thus, Easter Sunday begins a "new creation," a day on which this world is now redeemed and formed anew by Christ's Passion, Death, and Resurrection. "Therefore, if any one is in Christ, he is a new creation; the old has passed away, behold, the new has come" (2 Cor 5:17, RSVCE).

This world is now reconciled back to God after the fall of man in the Garden of Eden severed the relationship. Easter Sunday is now considered Day 1, the first day of a new creation where Christ has opened the doors to paradise through the merits He won for us at Calvary. If we can now say that Easter Sunday is the first day of a new creation here on earth, then all is perfectly fine, right? Not exactly.

All of mankind has been redeemed, but not all man-
will be saved. Our human nature is still broken, and
struggle with concupiscence and the vice it causes
lt of original sin. We will still be tested, as Scripture
ssed is the man who endures trial, for when he has

stood the test he will receive the crown of life which God has promised to those who love him" (Jas 1:12, RSVCE). This means that the world is still in a mess of sorts as we still turn to sin and toward ourselves instead of our Creator, resulting in a world full of pain and suffering.

The good news here is that while sin is still a reality, we no longer have to face eternal death due to our sins. We can now be freed from the chains that Satan tries to shackle us with, as long as we "Ask" for God's mercy and forgiveness (remember your ABCs). Salvation now comes to us through the ransom Jesus Christ paid for us on the Cross. Nevertheless, we still have to go through this life of trial and testing, through this valley of tears, and carry our crosses, just as Christ did. But one day, all that will be over when we enter into eternity and are glorified in Heaven (we pray) as Christ was glorified after His Resurrection.

Now we can see that, since Easter is Day 1 of this new creation, we still have to persevere through the next "seven days," which are symbolic of our pilgrimage here on earth called *life*. Although we are redeemed, we are not in our true home with God just yet. Just as the Israelites, after their Passover liberation from slavery in Egypt, were wandering in the desert seeking the Promised Land, we are on the pilgrimage of life seeking our promised land, which is Heaven. One day, our pilgrimage in this natural realm will be over, and we will enter into the supernatural realm of eternity, which symbolically will happen on the "eighth day" of our journey to God. Everything we do in this life should be preparing us to be ready for that day.

The Bride Needs to Be Spotless

This eighth day is when Christ, the Groom, will come for His Bride — us, the Church. Remember that in keeping with Jewish tradition, every good Jewish man ultimately desires to take his virgin bride home to meet his mother and his father. In Christ's case, it is no different — He desires to to take His Bride home to Heaven to meet God the Father and Mary, His Mother. And according to this same tradition, the groom wants his bride to be spotless and pure. So when Jesus, the Groom, comes for His Bride on the eighth day for their nuptial ceremony in eternity, He also wants her to be "dressed in white," without stain or blemish.

The problem is that we are sinners, and God knows that none of us are completely spotless. Thinking in terms of speculative theology here, Jesus has a dilemma: He wants to come for His Bride and He wants her spotless, but odds are we aren't going to be in that condition. Our wedding garment (our soul) will likely have some stain. That stain will be either in the form of unforgiven sin or the temporal punishment that remains even after our sins have been forgiven.

That first possible stain, *unforgiven sin*, is easily washed away in Sacrament of Confession. When the priest says, "I absolve you from your sins in the name of the Father and of the Son and of the Holy Spirit, Amen," you are guaranteed forgiveness. The main reason we want to receive forgiveness sacramentally, and not simply confess our sins privately to God, is because Christ established the Sacraments to be administered through His Church.

Jesus had ultimate authority to forgive sins here on earth, but when someone has "ultimate" authority, they have the power to also delegate that authority. Thus, when Jesus said to His disciples, "Whose sins you forgive are forgiven and whose sins you retain are retained" (see Mt 16:19; 18:18; Jn 20:23), He gave to them and all who followed them in apostolic succession (see Acts) that authority to forgive sins in His name. Thus, Heaven has to follow the priest, and if that priest says you are forgiven, Jesus says it shall be so! When the priest absolves you, you are guaranteed forgiveness or Christ's granting of power would be meaningless!

The other stain we may have to deal with is the *temporal punishment* we are due that could remain on our soul even after our sin is forgiven. I use the word "punishment" hesitantly (mainly I use it because the Church does), since it may be easier to think of it as loving discipline from a caring father. Let's say that this father tells his son not to play baseball in the front yard because one of the windows in the house might get broken. The father then goes to work, the son's friends come over, and they convince him that one quick game of baseball will not result in any broken windows.

Sure enough, the boy hits a line drive right through a window just as his father had warned. Later, the dad comes home and sees the broken window, causing him much disappointment. Gently looking at his son, who has his head hung low, he softly but firmly says, "Son, I forgive you." But before the son can get too excited, the father lays down the *punishment* by saying, "Because I love you and want you learn a lesson from this, you're grounded for two weeks and you're paying for this out of your allowance."

You see, although our sins are forgiven, there are still consequences, because those sins don't affect only us, they affect the rest of the Body of Christ — and not only the Body of Christ, but the whole moral order of God's creation. As explained in Chapter One, sin creates a disharmony in God's universe; while the wound of sin is healed in Confession, the scar on the Body of Christ may still remain. If it does, we have temporal punishment remaining for our sins that must be remitted, either in this life or after our death (aka Purgatory).

Some of you may respond to this by saying, "Gee, I thought Confession was all I needed?" This is a good point to raise because this may, in fact, be true. Church tradition says that when we confess our sins, all of the *eternal punishment* due to sin (aka hell) is removed. In other words, we no longer face the fires of hell as long as we have made a valid Confession. But the temporal punishment is a different matter.

Although our sins were forgiven in the confessional, unless we made our Confession with perfect contrition, the temporal punishment due to those sins may remain. Perfect contrition is our repentance for sin that is motivated by faith and the love of God alone — unlike imperfect contrition, which arises from a less pure motive, such as common decency (believing that something is "just wrong" and not truly repenting out of love for God) or fear of hell. Thus, perfect contrition is not easy; in fact, it is quite difficult to consistently achieve. That is why many of us still have some temporal punishment remaining for our sins (which can be cleared, as I just mentioned, in this life or after death).

How do we get rid of this temporal punishment so that our wedding garment, our soul, is spotless when Christ finally comes for us on the "eighth day?" The Church gives us a couple of means to be cleansed of this kind of stain. One of the best known ways available to us is the gift given through the authority of the Church, known as a plenary indulgence.

Plenary Indulgences

One tremendous grace that is given to us through the treasury of the Church is the opportunity to gain a daily plenary indulgence. A plenary indulgence is a grace granted from the Church's treasury of graces, attached to *an act or prayer that remits all temporal punishment due to sins already confessed.* Remember, although our sins are forgiven in Confession, we must nevertheless repair the damage they have done to the moral order of God's universe and to the Body of Christ. As we have stated, our sins have consequences.

The word *plenary* means "full." Consequently, there are also opportunities for *partial* indulgences as well, which remit not all, but some of the temporal punishment due to sin. The Church teaches that we can obtain indulgences for ourselves or for one of the Holy Souls in Purgatory, but not for another living person.

Since indulgences require certain conditions to be completed in order to be fulfilled, many people incorrectly believe that indulgences are just Catholic "rules and regulations," as if every Catholic is obliged to seek indulgences. In fact, we don't have to practice them at all; they are like "extra credit," a way to gain additional graces for ourselves or a deceased loved one if we so choose.

Jesus said to St. Faustina, **"The souls in Purgatory are greatly loved by Me. They are making retribution to My justice. It is in your power to bring them relief. Draw all the indulgences from the treasury of My Church"** (*Diary*, 1226).

There are many acts and prayers by which we can obtain plenary indulgences, but I want to discuss what I call the "Big Four." I refer to them as such because these four plenary indulgences can be performed anytime, anywhere, and with no extreme effort required. They are:

1. *Adoration of the Blessed Sacrament for at least one half-hour.*
2. *The pious exercise of the Stations of the Cross.*
3. *Recitation of the Rosary inside a church, chapel, or with another person.*
4. *The devout reading or listening to the Sacred Scriptures for at least one half-hour.*[24]

We can only gain one plenary indulgence a day; however, there is no limit on the number of partial indulgences we can gain. Even if we fail to meet all the conditions for a plenary indulgence, we will still receive a partial indulgence for our efforts. In this way we can still remove some of the punishment we (or a Holy Soul) are due for past transgressions.

These four practices are sources of tremendous grace, whether we obtain the attached indulgences or not. We should make them a regular part of our spiritual lives, if we can.

To obtain a plenary indulgence, the Church states that we must fulfill certain conditions:

- Go to Confession within 20 days of the act (one Confession can be applied to several plenary indulgences).

- Receive Holy Communion (once for each time we perform the indulgenced act).

- Pray for the intentions of the Holy Father (for instance, offering an *Our Father*, a *Hail Mary*, and a *Glory Be* for his intentions).

Note that if we are in a state of grace, we can go to Confession up to 20 days before or after the indulgenced act, but if we are not in a state of grace, we must go to Confession within 20 days *before* the indulgenced act in order to receive Holy Communion worthily.

The final requirement for receiving the indulgence is to have no attachment to sin, even venial. This is not easy, but don't despair. Remember, these are extra graces, and we are not under the penalty of sin if we don't perform an indulgence perfectly.

Some Partial Indulgences

Partial indulgences are available in two situations: 1) when we don't perfectly meet all the criteria to receive a plenary indulgence attached to some act or 2) wherever the Church has not attached a plenary indulgence to a given act or prayer. So no matter what, when we try to obtain an indulgence, we will. It's just a matter of whether we gather all or only some of the graces available. Examples of pious acts that meet the conditions for obtaining a partial indulgence include:

- Making the Sign of the Cross
- Praying the Rosary privately (not in common with others)
- Raising one's thoughts to God in a pious way
- Adoring Jesus in the Holy Eucharist for a moment
- Teaching or attending a catechism class

- Fasting
- Venerating a saint on his or her feast day
- Giving alms (helping the poor or homeless)

These are just some of the many partial indulgences available to us as part of the Church Militant. I bet many of you never realized how many graces are available for doing pious acts we normally do anyway, if we simply ask!

Let's return now to plenary indulgences, which are valuable, but sometimes difficult to receive. As we mentioned, to remit *all* of the punishment due to sin, you must complete the three conditions listed above *and* have no attachment to sin, even venial. Do you sometimes eat too much? Do you struggle with impure thoughts? Do you find yourself often running your mouth a bit too much? If so, you may have some attachment to sin, and the requirement to remove these attachments is not always easily overcome.

In addition to plenary indulgences, the Bible tells us that prayer, fasting, and almsgiving are three ways to remit punishment due to sin as well. However, to receive the remission of all punishment, those acts must be done with perfect love. For example, if you *pray*, but your prayer is tinged with any self-interest (such as desiring in your heart that your will be done rather than God's will), that is not perfect love. If you *fast*, but you take more joy in losing weight than doing it solely for the love of God, that is not perfect love. Or if you practice *almsgiving* by donating to a local charity, but silently hope you will somehow be recognized, that is not perfect love. Once again, like a plenary indulgence, this sounds difficult to attain, and it is.

To summarize, to remove all of the temporal punishment due to us or a loved one in Purgatory through a plenary indulgence, we can have no attachment to sin. That is not easy. To remit all punishment through prayer, fasting, or almsgiving, we have to do it with perfect love. That is not easy. Another way to remit all temporal punishment is through perfect contrition in the confessional, being sorry for our sins purely out of our love of God and not fear of hell, but that is also not easy.

So back to the question: What are we to do if we want to have any chance of being spotless when Jesus comes for us? It seems very difficult, even impossible, given our broken human nature. But, in His infinite mercy, God has given us one more and very special way to become spotless: The Feast of Divine Mercy!

The Extraordinary Grace of Divine Mercy Sunday

For those unable to have all temporal punishment remitted in this life because they don't have perfect love, perfect contrition, or perfect detachment from sin, all hope is not lost. We can still become perfectly "clean," a bride without stain even in the midst of our brokenness. How? As mentioned above, Jesus gives us the best way of all: the extraordinary grace of Divine Mercy Sunday!

Specifically, He told St. Faustina:

> **On that day** [Divine Mercy Sunday], **the very depths of My tender mercy are opened. I pour out a whole ocean of graces upon those souls who approach the fount of My mercy. ... On that day, all the divine floodgates through which graces flow are opened** (*Diary*, 699).

Regarding the graces of Divine Mercy Sunday, Jesus told St. Faustina, **"The soul that will go to Confession and receive Holy Communion shall obtain complete forgiveness of sins and punishment"** (*Diary*, 699).

If you have ever wished you could wipe your slate clean and start over, this is your chance! Please read that passage above one more time. This is an extraordinary promise! All sins *and* punishment are removed by the grace of this one day, Divine Mercy Sunday, when we fulfill the conditions of a valid Confession and worthily receive Holy Communion. That's it! No other conditions were specified by Christ, so we can have faith that even the most hardened sinner, no matter how broken, can go to Confession, receive Holy Communion, have trust in God's mercy, and be completely wiped clean of all sin and punishment!

Please note that this offer of grace is applied to any Mass on Divine Mercy Sunday or the Vigil the night before. You do not have to attend a specific 3 p.m. prayer service or a Mass where the priest specifically mentions the graces of this day. Any Mass suffices. The important point to understand is that we need to be prepared to receive this amazing grace, this "extraordinary grace," that now prepares us to be spotless and without stain. Fully cleansed, our soul now has the opportunity, if we desire it, to be able to receive our Groom when He comes for us on this the "eighth day."

We can therefore see why Jesus demanded that this day, Divine Mercy Sunday, be placed on the eighth day of the Easter Octave, the day that represents a new beginning and entrance into eternity. After receiving the grace offered on this day, we are able to enter into eternity without blemish, fully prepared to be taken by Christ to Heaven, because no sin or punishment due to sin remains. It's all gone. This is beyond incredible, beyond imagination! Only a God so loving and so merciful could grant us such an amazing grace!

An important point needs to be made here: I am often asked if these graces apply to one's whole life, past, present, and future. Unfortunately, no. This extraordinary promise cleanses us of everything up to and including your last participation in Divine Mercy Sunday. However, if you sin in the days following this day of mercy, the graces from that past Divine Mercy Sunday do not apply to those subsequent sins. You have to wait for the following year to be cleansed in the same way. Don't be discouraged, however, as this is still a prodigious gift beyond our comprehension.

In fact, this extraordinary promise of Divine Mercy Sunday is so great that it has been compared to the grace of Baptism. Father Seraphim Michalenko says it is "like" a *second* Baptism, because other than at the moment of our original Baptism, our soul will never be cleaner. Of course, this assumes we fulfill the conditions Jesus gave St. Faustina of going to Confession and receiving Holy Communion. On that day, Christ wipes away all sins and provides for the removal of all punishment due to sin (even for sins we forgot to confess, unlike a plenary indulgence), and this grace is fully effective even if our contrition is less than perfect, even if we don't have perfect love, and even if we still struggle with some attachment to particular sins.

What is required is receiving Holy Communion worthily, in a state of grace, with trust in Jesus' promise. As discussed thoroughly in previous chapters, trust is the key. What Jesus wants is for us to trust in Him and come to Him without fear of our sins. When we do, our souls are completely renewed!

It is important to point out, however, that this grace is not automatically effective without any effort on our part. We cannot have the intention to remain living in a state of sin with no desire for conversion. If we are living in a perpetual state of mortal sin, we need to do whatever possible to break free of the grip Satan has on us. When we do, we can then open the doors of our hearts to receive God's grace. It is imperative that we do this, because His grace is only fully received if we have some rectification of the will (similar to firm purpose of amendment), meaning that we are sorry for our past sins and will at least try to amend our lives. It doesn't mean that we will be perfect, it only means that we will try our best. This change of heart is necessary to receive the graces of Divine Mercy Sunday.

Even non-Catholics or homebound Catholics who cannot get to the Sacraments because their churches are closed can receive this grace if they desire it. If they truly ask God for forgiveness of their sins by making an Act of Contrition and want to be united to God by making an Act of Spiritual Communion, we believe God will grant this grace of His mercy (see *Catechism*, 1452).[25] But the surest, most guaranteed way to receive the grace of Divine Mercy Sunday is through the physical reception of the Sacraments, if possible.

That's what Divine Mercy Sunday is all about: simply a return to the Sacraments. It is not a magic wand or a rabbit's foot; it's the power of God's grace received through the Sacraments. On this day, we receive those graces as well as the removal of all temporal punishment. So if you have been away from Confession and Holy Communion for a while, you now have the ultimate incentive to return!

To receive the grace of Divine Mercy Sunday, you simply need to go to Confession before or on Divine Mercy Sunday — even sometime during Lent suffices. The important point is that you be in a state of grace on that day, meaning that you are aware of no mortal sin on your soul. Then you need to receive Holy Communion with the intention of obtaining this promised grace.

This is easy to do: As you prepare to receive Holy Communion at any Mass on that Sunday or the Vigil the night before (or making a spiritual communion), offer up a prayer like this:

> Lord Jesus Christ, Son of the living God, You promised St. Faustina that the soul that has been to Confession [I have] and the soul that receives Holy Communion with trust in Divine Mercy [I am] will receive the complete forgiveness of all sins and punishment. Lord, please give me this grace. Jesus, I trust in You.

Make that prayer with complete trust in Jesus and the sincere intent to turn away from sin, and Jesus will give you this grace! In fact, He *has* to, otherwise it would mean He doesn't keep His promises — and nobody is going to claim that! This feast is for those of us who are broken and who may not have temporal punishment remitted because of attachment to sin, imperfect love, or imperfect contrition. And while this grace is only for ourselves and cannot be offered for a Holy Soul in Purgatory, the grace is available to everyone on earth! This grace is *perfect,* even though we are not. This grace is so powerful that it can open the door to Heaven, so don't let Divine Mercy Sunday pass you by!

A final point should be made about the incredible graces offered on this day. On Divine Mercy Sunday the Church also gives us the opportunity to receive a plenary indulgence attached to an act of worship of the Divine Mercy or participation in a Divine Mercy service on that same day (under the normal conditions), which we can offer for ourselves or for one of the Holy Souls in Purgatory. Since this plenary indulgence is different from the extraordinary promise of Divine Mercy Sunday described above, we Marian Fathers recommend that you do what we do on this day. Specifically, we each ask for the "extraordinary promise" for ourselves and then we fulfill the conditions for the plenary indulgence and we offer that for a Holy Soul. Wow, talk about such powerful graces from God given in such abundance on this one day!

Saint Maria Faustina Kowalska

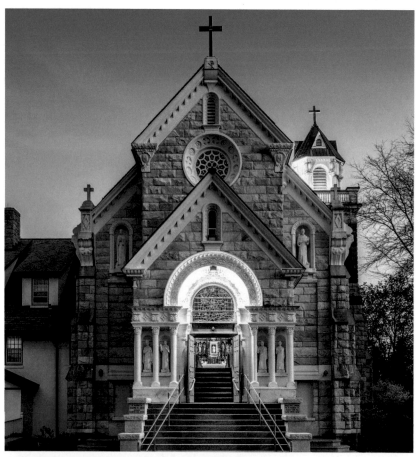

Two views of the National Shrine of The Divine Mercy,
Stockbridge, Massachusetts.

Divine Mercy Sunday procession to the altar of the
Mother of Mercy Outdoor Shrine.

Fr. Chris Alar, MIC

Life-size outdoor Stations of the Cross on the grounds
of the National Shrine of The Divine Mercy.

~ CHAPTER FOUR ~

The Image, Novena, Chaplet and Hour of Divine Mercy

As incredible as the grace of Divine Mercy Sunday is, it wasn't the first devotional channel of grace given by Jesus to St. Faustina. The first of the five channels of grace known as the *devotion to Divine Mercy* given by Christ was actually the Image of Divine Mercy.

The Image of Divine Mercy

The Image of Divine Mercy depicts Jesus as He appeared to St. Faustina when He physically came to her on Feb. 22, 1931. But before I continue with this point, I'd like to share an endearing story. After my ordination to the priesthood, my father began practicing his faith more than ever before. For a tough Marine who fought in Vietnam and never went deeper in his faith than attending Sunday Mass, it was quite amazing to see his spiritual growth. If that is due in part to graces given to my family from my answering God's call to be a priest, it is worth every bit of the sacrifice I made in giving up a career, a wife, and a family.

Since my father had been practicing his faith much more devoutly the past few years, I thought to myself, "You know, he might even know the answer to this little trivia question." It was Feb. 22, but I forget which year.

I said, "Hey, Dad, do you know what extremely important event happened on today's date? I'll give you a hint; it was truly a miracle." I was hoping that maybe he would know this was the day Jesus appeared to St. Faustina and showed Himself to her as we see in the Image of Divine Mercy.

He answered, "I sure do!"

Excited that this might be confirmation that he was truly growing deeper in his love of God and knowledge of Divine Mercy, I said, "Really?"

He said, "Yeah. It was the Miracle on Ice! This is the date the 1980 U.S. Olympic hockey team beat the Russians. One of the greatest days ever!"

Okay, Dad, that was surely a great day in our history, but it showed me that we still had a little more work to do on your faith journey! In any event, this memory always makes me chuckle.

As I mentioned previously, Feb. 22 is the day Jesus appeared to St. Faustina in her cell, in Poland back in 1931. He told her to have an image painted according to the pattern she saw before her (see *Diary*, 47). Can you imagine? You're St. Faustina. You return to your room from your work duties, close the door, turn around, and there is Jesus in your room! It wasn't just a locution or mental vision; He was physically present to her, as He would be standing in front of you or me.

Many times when people have a vision of Mary, no one else sees her; it's an internal vision. But not this time. Jesus was present to her in the flesh. How do we know this? In addition to St. Faustina telling us so, some sisters from her congregation recalled seeing light shining under her door at the time of her vision, light brighter than any candle could have emitted. Saint Faustina's convent did not have electricity, so there was no way that bright light was coming from an electric light. The only thing it could have been was an oil lamp. And one sister wrote that no oil lamp in the world could have made a light this bright.[26]

According to Fr. Seraphim, the convent chronicle also records that two of the girls in the sisters' care saw the lights shining from St. Faustina's window one evening, and went to the front door of the convent to inquire about it.[27] What was the light? It was coming from the red and pale rays emanating from Jesus' Sacred Heart, which was the source of the blood and water that gushed from His side after the Crucifixion.

This wasn't the only time Jesus' apparitions to St. Faustina were visible to other people besides St. Faustina. There's a story recorded in St. Faustina's *Diary*:

On Friday at ten minutes to six, when I and some of our wards were coming in from the garden to supper, I saw the Lord Jesus above our chapel, looking just as He did the first time I saw Him and just as He is painted in the image. The two rays which emanated from the Heart of Jesus covered our chapel and the infirmary, and then the whole city, and spread out over the whole world. This lasted about four minutes and disappeared. One of the girls, who was walking with me a little behind the others, also saw these rays, but she did not see Jesus, and she did not know from where these rays were emanating. She was overwhelmed and told the other girls. They began to laugh at her, suggesting that she was imagining things or that perhaps it was light reflected by a passing airplane. But she persisted in her conviction, saying that never had she seen such rays before. When the others suggested that it might have been a searchlight, she replied that she knew very well what a searchlight was like, but never had she seen rays such as these. After supper the girl approached me and told me she had been so moved by these rays that she could not keep silent, but wanted to tell everyone about them. Yet she had not seen Jesus. She kept telling me about these rays, and this put me in an awkward situation, as I could not tell her that I had seen the Lord Jesus (*Diary*, 87).

Just imagine how bright this light must have been; perhaps similar to a burst of light that must have been present at the moment of Christ's Resurrection. These stories demonstrate that St. Faustina was experiencing true external visions, not merely internal or intellectual visions.[28] Jesus was in some sense physically present to her on multiple occasions.

The Paschal Mystery

Pope Emeritus Benedict XVI once said that Christ is at the center of all true sacred art, and at the center of the image of Christ is the Paschal Mystery.[29] The Image of Divine Mercy captures this Mystery in the most vivid way. The reason for this is that the Paschal Mystery — the Passion, Death, Resurrection, and Ascension of Jesus — brought us our salvation. All the graces needed to save us are contained in this mystery.

The Paschal Mystery begins in the Upper Room on Holy Thursday, at the Last Supper, when Christ instituted the priesthood, the Eucharist, and the Mass. How do we see these things represented in the Image of Divine Mercy? First, by Jesus' attire. He is wearing a white robe called an *alb*, similar to what He would have worn at His trial under Pontius Pilate, and similar to what the Catholic priest now wears under his vestments for Mass. Jesus is dressed in the white linen vestment of the High Priest of the Jewish Temple.

Only the High Priest was allowed to wear this garment as he entered into the Holy of Holies of the Temple to offer the blood of the sacrificed lamb without blemish. Emerging from the inner sanctuary, he would raise his right hand and offer God's blessing to the people (see Lev 16:1-4; Sir 50:18-21). This Image powerfully manifests Jesus as the High Priest, who has offered the perfect self-sacrifice through which He has achieved redemption for all mankind. Moreover, St. Faustina saw Jesus barefoot, not wearing sandals, which is also something only the High Priest could do upon entering the Holy of Holies.

As the Book of Hebrews tells us, Jesus is the new High Priest, replacing the Old Testament High Priest (see Heb 4:14-10:18). He is now the one sacrificing, and the one being sacrificed, replacing the animal sacrifices that were used to atone for sin under the Old Covenant. As the High

Priest, He is offering Himself as the perfect Lamb to be slain for our sake, for our sin.

This sacrifice is once and for all; it is eternal. Thus, as the High Priest, Christ instituted the Eucharist as a memorial of His Passion and Death. This gives us a way on earth to partake in the eternal, sacrificial offering of His Body and Blood for our sins, and we partake in this at every Mass. That is why in the Image we see the red ray of His Most Precious Blood emanating from His Most Sacred Heart, along with the pale ray, symbolizing the cleansing waters of Baptism and Confession that wash away our sins. These are the same rays of blood and water that poured from our Lord's side on Calvary (see Jn 19:34).

The next event in the Paschal Mystery was Good Friday, and we all know what happened on that day: the Crucifixion. Although not clearly distinct in the Divine Mercy Image, the wounds of His Crucifixion are present on Jesus' hands and feet, showing the pain He endured while on the Cross.

What happened next in the Paschal Mystery? Easter Sunday, the day Jesus rose from the dead and redeemed the world. In the Divine Mercy Image, Christ is risen and His body is in a glorified state. He's depicted as He would have appeared walking into the Upper Room where the disciples were gathered on Easter and on the first Sunday after Easter (see Jn 20:19-23, 26-29). He is also depicted as coming out of the darkness, proceeding out of the Holy of Holies and into the Cenacle, known to Catholics as the "Upper Room," basically the very first church established by Christ.

We know that 40 days after the Resurrection marked the Ascension of Jesus into Heaven, when He was seated at the right hand of the Father. How is the Ascension captured in the Image? The Bible tells us that before Jesus ascended to the Father, He blessed all those present (see Lk 24:50). The traditional form of Jewish blessing was to raise your right hand to shoulder height. That's what we see Jesus doing in the original version of the Image, so He is blessing you every time you come before this Image. According to the Old Testament, the Jewish High Priest was also to emerge from the Holy of Holies on the Day of Atonement with his hand raised in blessing for all God's people, so even that is fulfilled in this amazing icon.

Ten days after the Ascension (50 days after Easter) was Pentecost. Although technically not part of the Paschal Mystery, this event is critical in the history of the Church. It was when the Holy Spirit descended upon Mary and the Apostles in the Upper Room, emboldening them to go and preach the Word of God with conviction. This was their "confirmation," when they were set aflame with fortitude to go and preach to both Jew and Gentile. This was the birth of the Church — born of blood (the Precious Blood) and water (forgiveness of sins). In this Image, the blood and water represent the Cross of Christ on Good Friday and the gift of the Holy Spirit on Pentecost. After this moment, the world would never be the same.

The Meaning of the Rays

The significance of these two rays cannot be overstated. When St. Faustina asked the Lord about them, He told her:

> **The two rays denote Blood and Water. The pale ray stands for the Water which makes souls righteous. The red ray stands for the Blood which is the life of souls...**
>
> **These two rays issued forth from the very depths of My tender mercy when My agonized Heart was opened by a lance on the Cross** (*Diary*, 299).

The graces flowing to us through the rays of blood and water defeat Satan's only two weapons: *sin* and *death*. Satan's first great tool, sin, is wiped away by the cleansing

waters of Baptism and the healing words of Confession. His second great tool, death, is wiped away by *life* — and life to the Jews was in the **blood** of the creature. Blood provides us life, so we receive life in Holy Communion by receiving the true Body and Blood, Soul and Divinity of Jesus.

To sum it up, these two rays represent what Christ asks us to do on the Feast of Divine Mercy Sunday: Go to Confession and receive Holy Communion. Recall the prayer Jesus gave to St. Faustina: "O Blood and Water, which gushed forth from the Heart of Jesus as a fount of mercy for us, I trust in You" (*Diary*, 84). This is why Jesus told St. Faustina that **"these rays shield souls from the wrath of My Father. Happy is the one who will dwell in their shelter, for the just hand of God shall not lay hold of him"** (*Diary*, 299).

We should note here that this statement by Jesus doesn't mean that the Father is the "angry and insensitive" God of the Old Testament while Jesus is the "nice and easy-going" God of the New Testament. No, they are the same God. What Jesus means here is that the wrath of the Father will strike at sin, and if we are holding on to that sin when the Father strikes, we will also get zapped. That is why we need to detach ourselves from sin, which is also the last condition for a plenary indulgence as described in Chapter Three.

Now let's return to the rays of blood and water emanating from Jesus' Heart. Doesn't Scripture tell us that both blood and water flowed out of the *side* of Christ? (See Jn 19:34.) Yes, so then how do we explain the apparent contradiction, with the rays in this icon coming not from His side, but from His Heart?

One of our employees here at the National Shrine of The Divine Mercy, a theologian named Dr. Robert Stackpole, has studied this very topic for years. As he explains, Roman soldiers were trained executioners and knew exactly where to place their spear into the side of an enemy on the battlefield, or a criminal on a cross. They knew exactly between what two ribs to slide that spear, pushing it through the chest cavity to puncture the heart, causing instant death.

The blood and the water that flowed out of Jesus' side, then, really came from His pierced Heart. This hypothesis seems to be supported by science, as scientists who studied the Shroud of Turin (believed by many to be the burial cloth of Christ) have found that the stain on the right side of Christ's body in the Shroud image actually came from the Heart. It is composed of the same fluids described in John's Gospel: blood and water.[30]

Connection to the Sacred Heart

I remember once being told by a good, older Jesuit priest, "All you need is the Sacred Heart. You don't need anything else. Don't waste your time!" Well, I agree that devotion to Jesus starts with the Sacred Heart, but if you believe the words of Jesus, it doesn't end with the Sacred Heart. It ends with the Divine Mercy message and devotion. As another older Jesuit also once said, "The Divine Mercy completes and fulfills the Sacred Heart. Divine Mercy does not replace the Sacred Heart message and devotion — it complements and completes it." In a way, we literally see this since the rays themselves come from the Sacred Heart and are a product of that Heart's love.

When Jesus appeared to St. Margaret Mary Alacoque in the 17th century with revelations of His Sacred Heart, He was coming in response to Jansenism. This heresy was particularly damaging to French culture at the time, portraying God as an "ogre," ready to strike and punish mankind for even the smallest of sins. Man began to fear God more than ever, becoming so scrupulous that the prevalent belief became one of "nobody can be saved." The idea of God being *love* was all but lost, replaced by a fear of a distant God who only wanted to crush and condemn all mankind.

In response to this problem, Jesus told St. Margaret Mary to tell the world, "I am Love, come to Me," desiring that people would approach Him with trust, not fear. But the wounds of original sin still ran deep, and mankind did not come to the Lord as a loving Father.

Never giving up on His beloved creatures, God kept calling them to Himself. This effort reached new heights in the beginning of the 20th century, when the Lord's pleas for mankind to accept His love were manifested through the Divine Mercy revelations to St. Faustina (see Chapter Two). What Jesus revealed to her would build upon the idea that "God is love" and take it even further — it would display the love of God being put into action.

We have defined mercy as *love in action*. This is why we can say when we encounter the love of God, it is an active love, a love that is real and concrete, constant yet moving, always seeking us and drawing us to Him. This is mercy.

As mentioned, the Image of Divine Mercy shows Jesus' devotion to us, manifested in His stepping forward, putting His love into action by proactively seeking us out. The reason we can trust Him and accept this invitation of His love is because of *what* and *who* He represents. As we discussed, we all come from the Father and we pray fervently to return to the Father (*exitus et reditus*), so we can fulfill our purpose in life and then be "happy with Him forever in heaven" (see the *Baltimore Catechism*).[31] This is the job of the Son, Jesus — to bring redeemed mankind back to the Father. To do that, He desires to rescue us and return us to where we belong.

Here it is helpful to make one more point: If the mercy of the Father could be encapsulated and shown to the world, it would be a great encouragement to our faith. It would help us to be able to visualize that mercy. It would allow us to trust Him more and to accept Him. Well, we can visualize it — it is the very same Image of Divine Mercy we are now discussing. As Pope Francis explains in his papal bull *Misericordiae Vultus* (*The Face of Mercy*), published on Divine Mercy Sunday 2015, Jesus Christ is "the face of the Father's mercy." Wow, the extent to which God will go to save us through His Divine Mercy is beyond our comprehension. This point is underscored by the final detail of the Image I'll discuss — the placement of His foot.

In the Image of Divine Mercy we see Jesus' left foot stepping forward as He is coming out of the darkness to come for us. It is also symbolic of Christ's return at the end of time, when He will come for His bride. Unlike the "deities" of many of the world's religions, our God is not a transcendent, unapproachable God; He humbled Himself so much that He condescended to become one of us and to be united to us.

We don't have to dedicate our lives searching for a hidden god like those revered in other religions. Our God has fully revealed Himself to us, became one of us, and is now on the move to come and find us — the Good Shepherd is coming to save His lost sheep. He's making His last-ditch effort before the end to reach you, as portrayed in this Image. Take His hand, grip it tight, and accept His mercy while there is still time!

Versions of the Image

There are many versions of the Divine Mercy Image, so I am often asked if one rendition is better than another. You probably have a favorite. Many people wonder, "Which of these different Images is the best one?" And the answer is there isn't necessarily a "best" one. So long as they are faithful to St. Faustina's description in her *Diary*, all of the Images include the fullness of the promises our Lord made, all being great channels of grace. As Jesus told St. Faustina, the significance of the Image is not in the color or in the brush, but in His mercy (see *Diary*, 313).

Always keep in mind that we don't worship the canvas or the paint or the Image itself — we worship what it represents: Jesus, the Divine Mercy. We are worshiping Christ who appears in the Image. In Exodus 20, God's commandment against graven images (that picture on your desk is a graven image, for example), is meant to put a stop to the *worship* of false idols, not necessarily having images in one's possession. Remember, God commanded Moses to carve a bronze serpent in the desert for the sick people to gaze upon to be healed (see Num 21:8) and He commanded Moses to make two gold cherubim for the Ark of the Covenant (see Ex 25:18-22).

The Israelites were disciplined by God because they worshipped the golden calf rather than God Himself. This is certainly not a danger when we speak of venerating the Image of Divine Mercy — to venerate the Image simply means to *honor* it. In the Image of Divine Mercy, we worship He whom the Image represents: Jesus Christ, the Second Person of the Trinity. "He who has seen me has seen me has seen the Father" (Jn 14:9, RSVCE).

As St. John Damascene pointed out, when God Himself is the One who makes images of heavenly realities through Scripture and especially through His Incarnation, we are free to (and ought to) copy those images, so to speak, and use them as aids to prayer and worship.[32]

Jesus confirmed this when He said to St. Faustina:

> **I promise that the soul that will venerate this image will not perish. I also promise victory over [its] enemies already here on earth, especially at the hour of death. I myself will defend it as My own glory** (*Diary*, 48).

He added:

> **I am offering people a vessel with which they are to keep coming for graces ... . That vessel is this image with the signature, 'Jesus, I trust in You'** (*Diary*, 327). Jesus also promised, **"By**

means of this image, I shall grant many graces to souls (*Diary*, 742).

Protection Through the Image

We have received countless testimonies of healing, protection, and conversions through the Image of Divine Mercy. The amount of letters we have received detailing powerful graces people have experienced over the years is nothing less than amazing. If you want to read about one of these incredible stories, Google "Ron Ragelis Hurricane Sandy," and you should find his story on our official website, TheDivineMercy.org. Ron sent us pictures to corroborate his story and they were quite compelling.

Before Hurricane Sandy roared up the east coast of the United States in 2012, people were evacuating from Ron's neighborhood on Long Island. While most everyone was urgently preparing to flee the area, he stopped and realized he needed to do one last thing. Ron took the Image of Divine Mercy, held it up to the storm, and consecrated his home to Jesus, the Divine Mercy. He then left the Image in the house and evacuated. A week later he returned to see all the houses in that neighborhood had been damaged: Their roofs had been crushed by trees, their windows had been broken, and many had been ruined by flooding. Ron's house, however, was completely untouched.

Another way to obtain promised protection with the Image of Divine Mercy is by hanging it on the door of your home. Jesus promised many graces for those who do so. Thus, we Marian Fathers urge you to put a blessed Image of Jesus, the Divine Mercy on your front doors (facing outward), to express your trust in the Lord's promise of protection. (You can search "Let's Seal the Doorposts" on YouTube.com and see our viral video on this topic.)

If you are unable to have the Image blessed by a priest, the Church surprisingly allows you to invoke a blessing yourself. The *Catechism* teaches that lay people may administer certain blessings on account of their baptismal priesthood (1669). How can you invoke such a blessing upon the Image of Divine Mercy? While making the Sign of the Cross over the Image, say: "Oh, Lord, I seek your blessing upon this Image, in the name of the Father, Son, and Holy Spirit, Amen."

In the spring of 2020, as the repercussions of the coronavirus became crystal clear, we prayed in the Easter Vigil preface to let the blood of the one true Lamb anoint our doorposts. This is a reference to Exodus 12:21-23, where God commanded the Israelites to seal their doorposts with the blood of a lamb so that the angel of death could pass over the houses that had been marked.

Jesus is now the sacrificial Lamb of God, and by offering Himself as atonement for our sins and those of the whole world through the outpouring of His Blood, He freed us from eternal death and sealed us for eternal life. If the blood of an animal, placed on the doorposts of Jewish homes, caused the angel of death to "pass over" those homes, how much more effective will be the blood of the true Lamb, Jesus Christ, placed on our doors?

We urge you, then, to put the Image of Divine Mercy with the inscription *Jesus, I Trust in You* upon your doors, as many have done in times of calamity. While this act of faith may not guarantee your family won't be physically affected by any illness or calamity, it will guarantee that by your trust in Jesus, you will obtain His promises of love and mercy, which will surround you and remain in you forever.

Blessed Michael Sopocko, St. Faustina's confessor, recalled that Jesus said, "Let everyone procure for their homes this Image because there will yet come trials. And those homes, and entire families, and everyone individually who will hold this image of mercy in deep reverence, I will preserve from every sort of misfortune. The time will come when all those who do so will give witness to the miraculous efficacy and to the special protection of mercy flowing from this Image."[33]

Sopocko recalled additional promises our Lord made through St. Faustina regarding the Image: "When chastisements for sins come upon the world and your own country will experience utter degradation, the only refuge will be trust in My mercy. I will protect the cities and homes in which the Divine Mercy Image is found; I will protect the persons who will venerate [honor] this Image. The only refuge will be trust in My Mercy."[34] In light of today's civil unrest, political divide, and international riots, I find these words to be of particular importance.

Maybe that is why our Lord told St. Faustina, **"By means of this Image I shall be granting many graces to souls; so, let every soul have access to it"** (*Diary*, 570).

We hear miraculous stories all the time regarding this living icon of Christ Himself. For example, at the end of World War II, when Adolf Hitler obliterated the city of Warsaw, Poland, in punishment for the Warsaw Uprising, there were approximately four buildings left standing in a particular section of the city. Every one of those structures had the Image of Divine Mercy inside. So get this Image, even if you have to draw a picture of it, or simply use a small prayer card. God will accept that. Enthrone it in your home, carry it in your wallet, and set it on your desk at work. This is a powerful means of grace.

Novena of Chaplets/
The Divine Mercy Novena

The next channel of grace given by Jesus to St. Faustina was the Divine Mercy Novena. A novena (from the Latin *novem*, or "nine") usually consists of nine consecutive days of prayer requesting a specific intention of God, commonly through the intercession of a particular saint. The tradition of praying novenas originated when Mary and the apostles prayed in the Upper Room during the nine days between Ascension and Pentecost. Those nine days of prayer, which culminated in the descent of the Holy Spirit, strengthened their belief in the power of prayer, the primary way of invoking God's grace and mercy.

Praying a novena can also give us confident hope that prayer has power and that when offered up with expectant faith, it will be heard and answered by God. It should be noted, however, that while all prayer is answered by God, it is not always answered in the way we want. God always knows what is best for us, and far more than we do!

There seems to be a novena for every occasion; for example, we would pray a novena to St. Anthony if we lose something or we would pray a novena to St. Peregrine for those who have cancer. But the novena to the Divine Mercy is different from other novenas because it is the only novena we have in the Catholic Church that is not based on our intentions, but rather on God's intentions. If you lose something, it's your intention to get it back. If you have cancer, it's your intention to ask for healing. Those are good prayer requests, and God always encourages us to pray to Him for just such reasons, but surprisingly they may not always be God's will.

This novena, however, was given directly to St. Faustina by Jesus with His specific intentions. It began on Good Friday and finished nine days later, on the Saturday before Divine Mercy Sunday (novenas typically end the day before the feast). Jesus told St. Faustina that the Chaplet of Divine Mercy is also to be offered every day as part of the novena. (See "How to Pray the Chaplet of Divine Mercy" on page 173.)

For each day of the novena, He asked that a different group of people be entrusted to Him:

DAY 1:

"**Today, bring to Me all mankind, especially all sinners.**" (Jesus told Faustina that praying for sinners consoled Him from the grief He felt at losing souls. See *Diary*, 1210.)

DAY 2:

"**Today bring to me the souls of priests and religious.**" (These souls gave Jesus strength to endure His Passion. See *Diary*, 1212.)

DAY 3:

"**Today bring to Me all devout and faithful souls.**" (These souls consoled Jesus on the Way of the Cross. See *Diary*, 1214.)

DAY 4:

"**Today bring to Me the pagans and those who do not yet know Me.**" (Jesus was thinking of these souls during His Passion. See *Diary*, 1216.)

DAY 5:

"**Today bring to Me the souls of heretics and schismatics.**" (When these souls are reunited with the Church, the wounds of Jesus' Passion are lessened. See *Diary*, 1218.)

DAY 6:

"**Today bring to me the meek and humble souls and the souls of little children.**" (These souls most closely correspond to Jesus' Heart. See *Diary*, 1220.)

DAY 7:

"**Today bring to me the souls who especially venerate and glorify My mercy.**" (None of these souls will go to hell, and Jesus will defend them when they die. See *Diary*, 1224.)

DAY 8:

"**Today bring to Me the souls who are in the prison**

of Purgatory." (Jesus says it is in our power to relieve these souls. See *Diary*, 1226.)

DAY 9:

"Today bring to Me souls who have become luke-warm." (These souls wound Jesus' Heart very painfully. See *Diary*, 1228.)

We should point out that these are the intentions given by Jesus specifically to St. Faustina and that we do not necessarily have to pray for these same intentions during the novena. Jesus gave this novena to Faustina to be prayed especially on the days between Good Friday and the Saturday before Divine Mercy Sunday, but we can pray it any time during the year. In other words, we can pray the novena exactly as Jesus instructed St. Faustina, or we can choose to do our own novena of chaplets, praying during any nine consecutive days of the year for any intention we desire. We usually refer to the former as "The Divine Mercy Novena" and the latter as "The Novena of Chaplets." The only requirement for both would be to include the praying of the Divine Mercy Chaplet during each day of the novena.

While you don't have to pray this Novena to obtain the grace of Divine Mercy Sunday, it is a good way to prepare. Jesus promised, **"By this novena** [of Chaplets]**, I will grant every possible grace to souls"** (*Diary*, 796). Scripture tells us that one of the main ways that prayer is efficacious is when it demonstrates our perseverance (see the parable of the Persistent Widow, Lk 18:1-8). A novena is an excellent way to show God such perseverance, and to demonstrate how much we desire His assistance. But don't get frustrated if you don't pray the novena perfectly. If you forget a certain element of the prayer or even miss a day, just resume it the next day and offer the intention with that much more love and prayerful zeal.

Novenas Work

I want to tell a quick story that shows the power of novenas, which goes back to the days when I lived in Charlotte, North Carolina. At that time, I was good friends with a lovely couple named Dom and Barb, and I never missed the chance to sneak a free meal with them whenever the opportunity arose. While both of them were beautifully devoted to their Catholic faith, Barb seemed to set a new standard in devotion to the saints. She loved all the saints and always invoked their intercession.

One day while at dinner, Barb proceeded to tell me the story about a bracelet that was given to her by her little granddaughter, Alexa. This bracelet had no monetary value, but it had much sentimental value because Alexa made it for her by hand with much love; so needless to say, Barb never took it off.

One day she was in the kitchen and was shocked to suddenly realize that the bracelet was no longer on her wrist. Obviously, she wasted no time in beginning a novena to St. Anthony, the patron of finding lost items. She diligently prayed to him for nine straight days, and guess what happened after she completed the novena? Nothing!

She then prayed another nine-day novena, just in case St. Anthony didn't hear her the first time. Again, nothing. Getting desperate, she began saying, "I'm going to trust, I'm going to trust." So she really got into the novena once again, thinking the third time would be the charm. When she reached the ninth day, she went to bed and said to St. Anthony, "Saint Anthony, I trust you. I'm shutting off the light, and when I wake up tomorrow, I totally expect that bracelet to be on this nightstand." She shut off the light. Guess what was there when she woke up? Nothing!

Barb was fuming. She stood up and said, "Saint Anthony, we are through! We're done! That's it. I prayed to you three times. I trusted you. You were supposed to find it. You know how much that bracelet meant to me!" She was crying in sad disbelief that apparently her faith wasn't strong enough to have this prayer answered. She went into the kitchen to begin her day, a day she believed would be filled with saddened defeat.

Trying to distract herself, she began to make Dom some pancakes for breakfast. Taking the pitcher filled with pancake batter in her hands, she inadvertently dropped it, and the ensuing mess was one for the ages. The batter went everywhere, running across the range top and down into the burners. In her mind, an already bad day had just gotten worse. Realizing her frustration, Dom immediately came over to assist, but quickly saw that cleaning the top of the stove with a towel would not suffice as it normally would. He got his tools and proceeded to remove the burners and disassemble the range top so that all of the batter could be cleaned.

While cleaning the mess that originally seemed to serve no purpose other than aggravation and a trial in patience, a discovery was made. Guess what Dom found? You guessed right: the bracelet! It had somehow fallen off Barb's wrist and down into the stove while she was in the kitchen a few weeks earlier. Had she not spilled the batter, she never would have found that precious bracelet. God works in mysterious ways, especially when saints are involved!

Dom picked up that bracelet, and showing it to Barb, gave her a look with wordless scolding, basically saying, "See, I told you heartfelt prayers would work." Recognizing her momentary lapse in faith, she mumbled, "I'm sorry, St. Anthony. I found more than this bracelet today."

Wow, that's the power of prayer. That's the power of a novena. And remember, a novena of Chaplets can be done at any time, for any prayer intention (intentions that are always in union with the will of God as best we know it, of course).

Chaplet of Divine Mercy

Another powerful channel of grace given by Jesus to St. Faustina, the Chaplet of Divine Mercy, is prayed on ordinary Rosary beads. It's an easy prayer that only takes about eight minutes to pray. One of the reasons I think God gave it to us is that He knows we sometimes struggle with sloth and dryness in prayer, so at times when the Rosary may seem a bit too long (I know you never think that!), the Chaplet is a powerful devotional tool.

The Chaplet is a great intercessory prayer — and Jesus attaches many promises to it. He says:

> **Say unceasingly the chaplet that I have taught you. Whoever will recite it will receive great mercy at the hour of death. Priests will recommend it to sinners as their last hope of salvation. Even if there were a sinner most hardened, if he were to recite this chaplet only once, he would receive grace from My infinite mercy. I desire that the whole world know My infinite mercy. I desire to grant unimaginable graces to those souls who trust in My mercy** (*Diary*, 687; see also 1541).
>
> **The souls that say this chaplet will be embraced by My mercy during their lifetime and especially at the hour of their death** (*Diary*, 754).

This prayer was given by Jesus to St. Faustina as a way to hold back the hand of an angel that was ready to strike a town in Poland as a chastisement. Interceding desperately for her native land, she recorded this in her *Diary*:

> The words with which I entreated God are these: **Eternal Father, I offer You the Body and Blood, Soul and Divinity of Your dearly**

beloved son, Our Lord Jesus Christ for our sins and those of the whole world; for the sake of His sorrowful Passion, have mercy on us (*Diary*, 475).

The next morning, when I entered chapel, I heard these words interiorly: **Every time you enter the chapel, immediately recite the prayer which I taught you yesterday.** When I had said the prayer, in my soul I heard these words: **This prayer will serve to appease My wrath. You will recite it for nine days, on the beads of the rosary, in the following manner: First of all, you will say one OUR FATHER and HAIL MARY and the I BELIEVE IN GOD. Then on the OUR FATHER beads you will say the following words: "Eternal Father, I offer You the Body and Blood, Soul and divinity of Your dearly beloved Son, Our Lord Jesus Christ, in atonement for our sins and those of the whole world." On the HAIL MARY beads you will say the following words: "For the sake of His sorrowful Passion have mercy on us and on the whole world." In conclusion, three times you will recite these words: "Holy God, Holy Mighty One, Holy Immortal One, have mercy on us and on the whole world"** (*Diary*, 476).

Through the words of the Chaplet, God's justice was placated and the angel was rendered helpless in carrying out an act of chastisement for the sins of the people. Many have asked what sin caused the near chastisement. Surprisingly, we don't find the answer in the *Diary*; rather, we read it in an interview with Blessed Michael Sopocko:

She wrote in her *Diary*, that Jesus himself said, that he was to destroy one of the most beautiful

cities of our country like Sodom on account of
the crimes perpetrated there. Which having read
in her *Diary*, I questioned her, what did this
prophecy mean? She replied confirming those
things which she wrote, and replying to a further
question of mine: on account of what kind of sins
is God inflicting these punishments, she replied:
especially on account of the massacre of infants
not yet born, as the most grievous crime of all.[35]

Let this be a strong warning for us today to pray for
our nation and to pray for an end to abortion. In fact, Fr.
Seraphim Michalenko says that the reason Jesus gave us the
Chaplet of Divine Mercy was to end abortion. The words
of St. Faustina above as retold by her confessor testify to
this fact.

The "Next Best Thing" after the Mass

To understand why the Divine Mercy Chaplet has so many
graces attached to it, we have to consider its connection to
the Liturgy — and to do that, we need to look at the Rosary
as well. In fact, both the Rosary and the Divine Mercy Chaplet are actually extensions of the Mass. These two prayers are
so powerful that if you missed Mass, they are the "next best
thing" you can do to receive as many graces as possible. (Of
course, if it is a Sunday Mass you missed without a valid
reason, the next best thing to do is go to Confession!)

Now let's consider how the Rosary is connected to the
Mass. The Mass is divided into two parts: the *Liturgy of the
Word* and the *Liturgy of the Eucharist*. What do we do during
the Liturgy of the Word? We meditate on Scripture. And
what is the Rosary? It's not just a bunch of Hail Marys, but
rather a meditation on Scripture, specifically the mysteries of
Christ's life in the Bible.

The Rosary is also incredibly effective against the devil.
When I was 6 years old, my family was moving from Utah

to Michigan. Trying to help, but getting more in the way than anything else, I reached to unpack a particular box. What was inside that box caught my attention, so I inquired about the "string of beads" I discovered. I asked my mother, "Mom, what is this?" She answered, "That's a Rosary. But nobody prays that anymore." Considering it was the 1970s, her statement reflected part of the misunderstanding about Mary and the Rosary that resulted from Vatican II. So I said, "Should I throw it away?" My mom thought about it for a moment, and then she replied, "You know, why don't you keep it. Put it back in the box."

Fast forward almost 40 years and I am now a priest. They say when a person accepts their vocational call to be a nun or a priest, God will shower many graces upon their family. Without question my family received many graces after I was ordained. For example, my mom and dad hadn't prayed the Rosary for nearly 50 years, but that changed during one of my short annual visits home in the second year of my priesthood. I walked in the door, and sure enough, my mom was there praying the Rosary — and for my intentions, no less. Unbeknownst to her, guess which Rosary she was praying with? That same Rosary I'd found in the box decades earlier. That is grace!

But the interesting thing I noticed was her pace: rapid-firing on all cylinders, racing around the beads as fast as she could, repeating, "Hail Mary full of grace, the Lord is with thee ... Hail Mary full of grace, the Lord is with thee." I said, "Mom, stop. Stop! What is the Rosary? It's not just a bunch of Hail Marys. The Rosary is a meditation on Scripture. As you pray the Hail Marys, you're supposed to meditate on the mysteries, on the biblical events of the life of Christ. The Hail Marys are just background music. Like a good movie that has a powerful musical score, the music is not the focus; the music *focuses* you on the plot. And the Hail Marys help to focus us on the plot of the mysteries of Jesus' life."

God bless my mom. She said, "Wait a minute. I heard that every time you say a Hail Mary, it's like shooting a bullet into the devil!" She held up the Rosary, exclaiming, "And this is my machine gun!" Okay Mom, you got me on that one! But the point remains the same, in that the Rosary is similar to the first part of the Mass, the Liturgy of the Word.

Fittingly, the Chaplet of Divine Mercy is an extension of the second part of the Mass, the Liturgy of the Eucharist. That's because in this part of the Mass, the priest offers the sacrifice of Jesus' Body and Blood for the sins of the world. But that brings up yet another important question I am often asked. One of the big complaints we commonly hear from people is, "Father, how can I pray this prayer? It sounds inappropriate for me to pray 'Eternal Father, I offer you the Body and Blood, Soul and Divinity of Your Dearly Beloved Son, Our Lord Jesus Christ, in atonement for our sins and the sins of the whole world.' Who am I to pray that? I can't offer the Son to the Father. I'm not a priest. Father, you even said the Mass is *God* offering God to God with the priest being *in persona Christi*. I can't offer God to God. I'm not a priest."

Actually, you are. Vatican II tells us that, by virtue of our Baptism, we participate in the three offices of Christ: *priest, prophet,* and *king*.[36] You're a prophet. What does a prophet do? A prophet teaches. You are to teach your loved ones the ways of the Lord. You're a king. What does a king do? A king governs. You are to govern your family in the ways of the Lord and govern your body in the ways of health and holiness. But you're also a priest. Not a ministerial priest like me necessarily, but you share in the common priesthood of Christ. And what does a priest do? A priest offers *sacrifice*.

Thus, when you say, "Eternal Father, I offer you the Body and Blood, Soul and Divinity of Your Dearly Beloved Son, Our Lord, Jesus Christ," it just may be the best way to exercise your baptismal (or common) priesthood, by offering a spiritual sacrifice! This is why we can say this prayer and not deem ourselves unworthy of offering Christ to the

Father. It is amazing that God would allow us to share in such incredible graces.

If you should miss Mass, pray the Rosary and the Divine Mercy Chaplet, make an Examination of Conscience and an Act of Contrition for the forgiveness of sins until you can get to Confession, then pray an Act of Spiritual Communion asking God for the graces to receive Him in your soul as if you received Him in Holy Communion. Please don't misunderstand me, there is nothing better than attending Mass and receiving our Lord sacramentally. But due to reasons beyond our control, such as lockdowns or mandated quarantines, we are sometimes unable to attend Mass. In those situations, these prayers are the next best way to receive God's grace. Remember, while *we* are bound by the Sacraments, God is *not*.

Hour of Mercy (3 p.m.)

The final channel of grace pointed out by Jesus to St. Faustina was a very "timely" one. Because Jesus died on the Cross for us at 3 p.m., the hour between 3 and 4 in the afternoon is known as the *Hour of Great Mercy*. Jesus told St. Faustina that during this time, she should invoke His mercy for the world, particularly for the conversion of sinners. He also told her to pray the Stations of the Cross at this hour, provided her duties permitted it. If she couldn't do that, He asked her to briefly go into the chapel and adore Him in the Blessed Sacrament, and if that was not possible, to simply stop wherever she was and absorb herself in prayer, even if only for a moment, meditating on His Passion (see *Diary*, 1572).

Interestingly, Jesus never told St. Faustina to specifically pray the Chaplet of Divine Mercy at 3 p.m. Why then do we pray the Chaplet in the 3 o'clock hour? Because it is about His Passion. As the prayer states, "For the sake of His Sorrowful *Passion*, have mercy on us and on the whole world."

Jesus told St. Faustina:

> **As often as you hear the clock strike the third hour** [the hour of Christ's death], **immerse yourself completely in My mercy, adoring and glorifying it; invoke its omnipotence for the whole world, and particularly for poor sinners … . In this hour you can obtain everything for yourself and for others for the asking** (*Diary*, 1572).

What Jesus wants above all during this time is that *we* have mercy on Him! (See *Diary*, 50, 177). He wants us to recall His sacrifice of love. He wants us to think about what He did for us on the Cross, and to unite ourselves to His Passion.

Jesus also promised, **"This is the hour of great mercy for the whole world. … I will refuse nothing to the soul that makes a request of Me in virtue of My Passion"** (*Diary*, 1320).

Through St. Faustina Kowalska, our Lord specifically asked for acts of love for Him and for our neighbor. We are to commemorate the hour of His death on the Cross (see *Diary*, 1572) and to pray for the conversion of others at this time. I find it particularly motivating because there is much merit when we do:

> **There is more merit to one hour of meditation on My sorrowful Passion than there is to a whole year of flagellation that draws blood; the contemplation of My painful wounds is of great profit to you, and it brings Me great joy** (*Diary*, 369).

On a final note, sometimes people say to me, "Father, I'm always awakened at 3 a.m., the hour of the devil." Keep in mind that no hour of the day belongs to the devil, especially the 3 a.m. hour. The reason is because tradition tells us that Jesus rose from the dead at 3 a.m. Since many theologians believe Jesus did rise at this time, this hour, like all hours, belongs to Jesus Christ! It is not the devil's hour. And what's true about time is also true about your soul. You may have heard people say that someone "sold their soul to the devil." You cannot sell your soul to the devil, because you don't own it — God does. That doesn't mean you can't be insanely stupid and offer your life in service to Satan, but even if someone does such a misguided, unexplainable act, God still owns their soul and He still loves that soul forever. That is the fathomless mercy of God, which is His greatest attribute.

Summary of the Devotion to Divine Mercy (FINCH)

Hopefully it is now clear why John Paul II inferred that Divine Mercy is the most important message of our times.[37] This statement is true because of what Jesus told St. Faustina: **"I am giving mankind the last hope of salvation; that is, recourse to My mercy"** (*Diary*, 998).

What does "recourse" to God's mercy mean? It is what we have been talking about throughout this book. It means living the ABCs:

- **A**sk for God's mercy
- **B**e merciful to each other
- **C**ompletely trust in God's mercy

These three elements make up the message of Divine Mercy, and we need all three to get to Heaven. As mentioned in Chapter One, Pope Benedict XVI said the message of Divine Mercy is the "nucleus of the Gospel," and for this reason, the message is not optional; we cannot reject it. God has been showing us this blueprint for salvation throughout history, ever since Adam and Eve committed the original sin. After centuries of trying to get us to live this message, He raised up St. Faustina, a great saint, to renew the world in His Divine Mercy and to prepare us for His return.

In order to do this, our Lord gave her five new channels of grace known as the devotion to Divine Mercy, which can help us to live the message of Divine Mercy more strongly. We can remember these channels by the acronym "FINCH":

- The **F**east of Divine Mercy
- The **I**mage of Divine Mercy
- The **N**ovena of Chaplets
- The **C**haplet of Divine Mercy
- The **H**our of Divine Mercy

These five channels summarize what we need to do to have recourse to Divine Mercy. Practice the devotion to Divine Mercy in your life to receive the infinite graces that God has "died" to give you. Jesus said the flames of mercy are **"clamoring"** to be spent. He deeply desires to shower these graces upon us, and to **"immerse"** us in His infinite mercy (see *Diary*, 50, 177).

The *Diary* makes it clear that if all the sins ever committed were put together, they would be just a drop compared to the ocean that is God's mercy (see *Diary*, 1777). That is why John Paul II said, "There is nothing that man needs more than Divine Mercy — that love which is benevolent, which is compassionate, which raises man above his weakness to the infinite heights of the holiness of God."[38]

Recognizing the importance of this message and devotion, on Aug. 17, 2002, he entrusted the world to Divine Mercy at the dedication of the Sanctuary of Divine Mercy in Lagiewniki, Poland. His successor, Pope Benedict XVI, taught that Divine Mercy "is not a secondary devotion but an integral dimension of Christian faith and prayer."[39] And Pope Francis more recently declared an extraordinary Jubilee Year of Mercy in 2015-2016, reiterating the message from St. Faustina's *Diary* that now is the time of mercy (see *Diary*, 1588). We have to remember that while the mercy of God is infinite, the time of mercy is not. Since our last three popes have begged us to seek God's mercy, we need to heed that call.

We have the opportunity now to walk through the doors of God's mercy so that we will not have to go through the doors of His justice later. Through her writings, her prayers, her sufferings on behalf of poor sinners, and her steadfast love of God, St. Faustina is preparing the world for Jesus' final coming, a mission she herself said would continue after her death (see *Diary*, 281, 1582).

On Nov. 22, 1981, at the Shrine of Merciful Love in Collevalenza, Italy, John Paul II stated:

> Right from the beginning of my ministry in St. Peter's See in Rome, I consider this message [of Divine Mercy] my special task. Providence has assigned it to me in the present situation of man, the Church and the world. It could be said that precisely this situation assigned that message to me as my task before God.

If you think of all the things John Paul II accomplished, this was his most special task before God? To canonize this inconspicuous nun, to spread the Divine Mercy message and devotion, and to institute the Feast of Divine Mercy? This is an eye-opening revelation, one that needs to be taken into the depths of our soul. Regarding St. Faustina's canonization, on April 30, 2005, John Paul II addressed a private gathering with our Marian priests and brothers after the public ceremony, saying, "This is the happiest day of my life."[40] Wow, that's quite a statement considering all John Paul experienced during his time on this earth.

John Paul's life would culminate in the embrace of Divine Mercy. Cardinal Stanisław Dziwisz, who had been the pope's secretary and assistant for 40 years, shared an amazing story with our congregation when he came to the National Shrine of The Divine Mercy in 2014. He said that on the Saturday before Divine Mercy Sunday in 2005, John Paul II went to Confession and attended a morning Mass, and he was not planning to celebrate Mass again until the next morning, which was Divine Mercy Sunday. As the day progressed, the pope was getting weaker. Eventually it was after 5 p.m., when it is permitted to celebrate the Mass of Anticipation for Sunday — popularly known as the "Vigil Mass."

Cardinal Dziwisz says there were no plans to do this, however, because John Paul II was very sick. All of a sudden, it was placed on his heart to celebrate Mass with John Paul. At first, the Cardinal said he ignored it. Then an hour or so later, it was put on his heart again: "Celebrate the Mass for Divine Mercy Sunday with John Paul." He ignored it again. By now it was around 8:30 p.m., and a third time it was put on his heart: "Celebrate Mass for Divine Mercy Sunday with John Paul." Finally, he surrendered.

Can you imagine Cardinal Dziwisz rummaging through the sacristy, pulling out corporals, purificators, ciboriums, and chalices, and trying to set up an unplanned Mass on the spur of the moment? With only himself and John Paul II, he celebrated Mass for Divine Mercy Sunday. John Paul, who had been to Confession, then received Holy Communion for Divine Mercy Sunday, died 25 minutes later.

You don't believe that was the grace of God giving him the gift of being able to go straight to Heaven as the spouse of Christ? I certainly believe it was in honor of all he did to help spread Divine Mercy around the world. Regarding all those who venerated and glorified His mercy, Jesus told St. Faustina that He would **"particularly defend each one of them at the hour of death"** (*Diary*, 1224). I believe we can have confident hope that John Paul II died with all the promised graces Jesus gave regarding Divine Mercy Sunday.

In summary, let's remember that it was to the novice sister St. Faustina, considered "no one special" by her superior, that Jesus Christ quietly entrusted a great mission. Christ instructed Faustina to remind the world about God's unfathomable mercy. She was to accomplish this by introducing new devotional practices to honor mercy and by establishing a worldwide movement of souls dedicated to spreading Divine Mercy. Jesus directed Faustina to proclaim to the world that even the worst and most hopeless sinner was deserving of God's infinite mercy.

He told her:

Speak to the world about my mercy; let all mankind recognize my unfathomable mercy. It is a sign for the end times; after it will come the day of justice. While there is still time, let them have recourse to the fount of My mercy (*Diary*, 848).

The Lord has been prolonging the time of mercy for some time, probably due in part to the prayers, works of mercy, and sufferings offered up by faithful people like John Paul II and yourself. Jesus wants you to be with Him in Heaven and He wants you to be spotless so He can bring you there. There is no way you would be reading this if Jesus wasn't clamoring in His Heart to be united with you through His mercy, and now you have a chance to do it on this coming Divine Mercy Sunday. Please do. We never know when we will be called from this world. That, ladies and gentleman, is all God wants. He simply wants to shower you with forgiveness, love, and mercy and to get you to Heaven.

This is why Jesus said to St. Faustina, **"I have eternity for punishing ... and so I am prolonging the time of mercy for the sake of** [sinners]. **But woe to them if they do not recognize this time of My visitation"** (*Diary*,

1160). Now is the time of mercy. Thank God that you recognize it, or again, you wouldn't be reading this book! That is why we Marian Fathers, who have continued this mission of spreading the Divine Mercy message and devotion around the world, invite you to become a member of our Marian family and to join us in this incredible ministry of evangelization, even if you can't leave the confines of your own home. For more information on how to become a Marian Helper, please see the ad on page 181.

~ CHAPTER FIVE ~

God's Mercy in the Midst of Suffering and Loss

I realize that some readers may get to this point and say, "This all sounds great, and I believe God is love, but it is clear that He loves some people more than others. He filled St. Faustina with all kinds of consolations, but my prayers don't get answered, I don't feel His presence, and worst of all the sufferings and trials of my life have become unbearable. Frankly, where is God in the midst of all of this?"

Therefore, we would be remiss if we only discussed God's mercy in this book without explaining how such trials and suffering are allowed to occur. It is true, one of the most difficult challenges of our faith is trying to understand where to find God's mercy in the midst of suffering. Oftentimes, we cannot understand why a good and loving God would allow such pain and difficulty in our lives. In fact, ask any pastor or evangelist, and they'll tell you that from their experience, one of the main reasons people don't believe in God is because they think that if there was a God, He would not allow the human race to experience such evil, unrest, and suffering.

Even for those who do believe, suffering is problematic. Many religions believe that suffering is evil, that it must be some form of punishment from a vindictive God who is vexed with them for each and every transgression they have ever committed against His law. We can find this idea in the Old Testament as well. For example, one of Job's friends tells him that he must have committed some kind of terrible sin to be so harshly treated by God: "Is it for your fear of him that he reproves you, and enters into judgment with you? Is not your wickedness great? There is no end to your iniquities" (Job 22:4-5, RSVCE).

In one sense, we can understand that we will experience some afflictions in this life because, as we said, there are consequences for our sins, and many times those consequences are the very cause of our suffering. But our Catholic faith is unique, and many times paradoxical, because the saints tell us that suffering has inestimable redemptive worth that is unequaled by anything else.

However, if you try to talk to anyone in the midst of trauma and attempt to explain this, you'll often be met with a blank stare, verbalized confusion, or outright anger. So this is the question: How do we understand why a merciful God would allow so much suffering? Didn't we say earlier that mercy is the particular mode of love such that when this love encounters suffering, it takes action to do something about it? Yes, we did. But sometimes, counterintuitively, God's mercy is most seen when He allows that suffering to happen. When He does, it is always out of love. To explain why, we'll start with some of the basics.

Free Will and Its Consequences

Our faith teaches that one of the greatest gifts we received from God at creation was free will. We have been given full freedom to make decisions in our life, whether they are in obedience to God's will or not. Of course, there are a lot of choices we make daily that we need not be overly scrupulous about, such as preferring chocolate ice cream over vanilla ice cream (which I do by the way).

In other matters, however, our decisions have more serious implications. Here, God doesn't just leave matters of preference to us. He gave us the natural law and 10 Commandments to follow as our moral compass, even though we have the free will to obey His directives or not. We were given freedom to choose good or evil, love or hate, generosity or miserliness. While free will was one of God's greatest gifts to us, ironically it was also the one where He took the greatest risk — the enormous risk that we would use our freedom to reject His love and hurt one another.

Thus, when we make bad choices that will offend God, harm ourselves, or injure others, God will not always intervene to stop it. If He did that every time, His gift of free will would be rendered meaningless. If God never allowed our choices, even the ignoble ones, to play out, we would simply be "robots" rather than His children who have the ability to willingly choose to love Him. Without this gift of free will, our love of Him would be forced, rather than free, and thus would not be true love.

It is that free and loving response that God desires from us, but for it to be authentic, the possibility must exist for us to choose *not* to love Him and those people God puts in our path. That is one reason why suffering exists in the world — when we make those wrong (but free) choices against God and neighbor, there are consequences to our actions, and those consequences can cause us and the world much suffering.

With free will comes the reality that our decisions have ramifications, both good and bad. Many times we give into temptations, rationalizing to ourselves, "Well, this won't hurt anybody and it is something I really want to do." But remember, your sin in private affects me, and my sin in private affects you. When we sin, we disrupt the harmony of God's entire universe. Every sin we commit, even venial sin, wounds the Body of Christ, of which we are all a part.

As we explained earlier, the surest way to heal that wound is through the Sacrament of Confession, where God's mercy is showered upon us and we are reconciled back to Him. But even after the wound between us and God is healed in Confession, a scar remains on the Body of Christ and on the whole world. Thus, it is best if our sins are atoned for through prayer, penance, sacrifice, and other means. If they are not, these consequences may become manifest through such things as sickness, natural disasters, estranged relationships, and other negative effects.

These are all examples of the disorder our sins can bring into the world. Not only are our personal lives affected, but the lives of others are impacted, and even nature is affected in a negative way. This is yet another reason why there is suffering in the world. Sin is like poison spewed into God's universe, but atonement is like the medicine needed to remove it.

In Chapter One we discussed how evil is not a real or created thing, but rather a privation of the good. The consequences of removing God from our courts, from our schools, from our families, and from huge swaths of our society, is removing Goodness itself. When we make free will choices to remove God from our society, the lack of the good that results is called *evil*. Thus, much of our suffering that we think God is inflicting upon us is really the opposite. We are inflicting it upon ourselves by eliminating the very source of mercy who could bring about an end to that suffering.

This brings to mind the age-old question of whether or not God wants suffering to happen. If we have free will, is it even within God's control to stop the suffering that can result from our bad choices? To answer this, let's back up even further. Is everything that happens under the Providence of God? Yes, it is. Does that then mean that God *wants* a little 5-year-old girl to die of leukemia? No, it doesn't.

This sounds like a major contradiction. If everything is under the Providence of God, and He wants only the good for us, then why does He allow us to go through such pain? While we offered some reasoning for this above with the explanation of free will, there is an even deeper reason that will help us to answer this perplexing question.

God Wants to Bring a Greater Good

We have all asked these questions at one time or another: "*Where was God when I needed Him?*" "*Why did He let this happen? Isn't He supposed to be merciful?*" In His *ordained* will, God does not want evil and suffering in the world; He doesn't want us to be in pain or have to endure crippling sorrow. God doesn't want us to have to undergo the anguish of the 9/11 attacks, the coronavirus, or childhood cancer. Yet in a way we can't fully understand, He allows it. In His *permissive* will, God doesn't always stop our choices to do evil or the consequences that come from our sins.

The reason for this is that God wants us to see our need for His mercy and forgiveness so He can forgive us and be merciful to us. Moreover, He allows it so that He can bring a greater good out of even the worst evils. In this way, God doesn't have to compromise His prodigious gift of our free will, and at the same time He can show His extreme love and care for us. It makes beautiful sense when you think about it.

Even with this explanation, however, we encounter another paradox: *How can good come from evil?* Well, our Lord has always been the "Lord of the paradox": The last will be first, the poor will become rich, the hungry will be satisfied, and the persecuted will find justice. One of the greatest of the Beatitudes is the promise that those who are mourning will be comforted (see Mt 5:4). This is God telling us that He will pick up the pieces of any tragedy and that He wants to bring a greater good out of it. We may never know what exactly that good is, but we can trust that it will come about. It is also important to keep in mind that this "greater good" may not even be in this world, but in the world to come.

To illustrate this point, another quick story is in order. Shortly after my ordination to the priesthood, I was on the road doing a parish mission with then-Br. Allen Alexander, MIC, now Fr. Allen. We were in Chicago and had just finished our night of evangelization. It was a Sunday evening, and by the time we packed our belongings and exited the Church, it was getting quite late. We had about an hour drive through downtown Chicago to the far western suburbs, to our Marian parish where we were spending the night. We had not eaten all day, so to say we were hungry was an understatement.

Looking for something inexpensive and convenient, we noticed a White Castle hamburger restaurant, and we decided to go inside to eat. Upon entering the lobby area, we noticed it was quite crowded, with about 50 or 60 people present. We proceeded to get in line and examine the menu. As we were waiting our turn, a despondent man walked through the door and immediately fixed his gaze upon our Roman Catholic clerical collars.

Many times you can just tell when someone is suffering. But this man's suffering seemingly turned to outright anger when he saw us, precipitating his approach toward us. Anticipating some form of visceral reaction based on his clenched fists and grinding teeth, I started thinking, "*What's the church teaching on self-defense?*" I grabbed Br. Allen and threw him in front of me. (Allen is 6 foot 2, and I am not!) The man proceeded to take his two fingers and forcefully jam them into my collar in front of everyone, shouting, "You tell me *how* your God could allow my 5-year-old niece to die of leukemia!"

The whole place fell dead silent. I would guess that lobby included some people who hadn't been to a church in many years or even their entire life. There were drug addicts, prostitutes, and even homeless people of all kinds. These were truly the suffering souls of downtown Chicago, and this guy caught their attention with his question that demanded an immediate answer.

In response, I began in the best way I knew how — I started quoting the *Summa Theologiae* of St. Thomas Aquinas. As a freshly minted priest right out of seminary, I start telling him that the tragedy of his niece's death was a result of original sin, how evil is a privation of the good, and so on.

Needless to say, he wasn't ready for that. Neither was anyone else in the restaurant that night. He passionately exclaimed, "She had no sin! She was only 5 years old!" Oblivious to the pastoral need of the moment, I continued, "Sir, it's a consequence, not of her sin, but of my sin and your sin. You see, when we wound the Body of Christ ..." It went right over his head. Rather than targeting his intellect, what I needed to do instead was to reach his wounded heart. Enter Br. Allen.

Thank goodness my brother in Christ was there, because I was making a mess out of an incredible opportunity — a situation where everyone in this restaurant was ready to hear about God, if only for a brief moment. Brother Allen basically shoved me aside, and started to pick up my broken pieces.

"Sir," Br. Allen began, "what's your name?" I was standing back thinking, *"Gee, I should have thought of that."* The man mumbled softly, "Harold." Brother Allen then said, "Harold, do you believe in God?" He responded, "I don't know. I just don't know." Everyone in the place was listening intently.

Brother Allen continued, "Harold, I don't know you, but I can tell you right now there's a little 5-year-old girl sitting on the lap of Jesus, and I can promise you she's praying her little heart out for you because you're in her heart and she's in your heart. And I can promise you, there is no way Jesus won't hear that prayer. Now, that doesn't mean He will always answer prayers when we want or in the way we expect. But He will answer. That's a promise."

"Now you see, Harold, if I were a betting man, I would bet you that her little prayers are going to bring you back to God. Maybe not today. Maybe not tomorrow. Maybe not until the moment of your death. I don't know. But I believe those prayers will allow you to accept God's love and mercy, even in the midst of darkness. And when you do, we're going to have two saved souls. Hers is already saved. You are right, she had no sin. She was only 5 years old."

"That means she's in Heaven. We know that, and now with her prayers I believe one day you will join her. You see, Harold, if she had been raised in this crazy world of ours, well, maybe she would never have made it to Jesus. We don't know the way God works. His ways are not our ways. Maybe God knew something. I am sure that God in His infinite mercy will bring a greater good out of her illness and passing. I don't expect you to believe that. I don't expect you to understand that right now, but someday I think you will."

Brother Allen continued, "It is very possible that if she had grown up in this pagan world she may have fallen away. Maybe she would have had nothing to do with God and would have been lost, then right behind her, you too. But you see, Harold, I believe in my heart that both of you will now be saved. God knows better than we do, and we won't understand all of this until after we die. I can tell you this, however: God did not abandon you, and He certainly did not abandon your little niece."

After Br. Allen finished, everybody was listening and wondering how Harold was going to respond. With a tear in his eye, he put his head down and seemed to acknowledge Br. Allen's words. This man who was so angry had probably never heard anything like this before. Everybody present was dumbfounded. You could have heard a pin drop in that restaurant.

Harold then turned around and silently walked out the door without getting his food. That's how impactful the moment was. I always think of him and wonder what happened to him. I do pray for him, asking God to help alleviate some of the pain he is enduring as a result of such a difficult loss.

Did God want that little girl to die of leukemia? No, but He allowed it. Somehow we try to trust that God will bring good out of just such a situation. In this spectacular case, it was about the possible good of two saved souls rather than two potentially lost souls.

This story only makes sense if we believe in something greater than what we experience here on earth. If we don't have faith in a life beyond this world, then suffering makes no sense and has no value. God permits evil and sin so that we may know His mercy is greater than sin and death. This gives God more glory than if we had never sinned in the first place. This is why we hear the phrase "O happy fault" at every Easter Vigil, referring to the fall of Adam and Eve; God actually brought a greater good out of something as tragic as the fall in the Garden of Eden. The greater good was the redemption of mankind and the elevation of human nature through the Passion, Death, and Resurrection of Jesus Christ.

The Mercy of Suffering

Now let's look a little deeper into the meaning of the phrase "O happy fault." When Adam and Eve were in the Garden of Eden before the fall, things were good, as they lived in perfect harmony with each other and with all of creation. They had preternatural gifts, meaning that they didn't get sick, they didn't suffer, and they knew no sin or shame.

When God breathed the breath of life into Adam, He shared with him His Spirit. Adam and Eve had sanctifying grace before the fall, truly being made in the image and likeness of God. They were, Scripture tells us, God's children (see Gen 1:26; 5:3; Lk 3:38) by grace, but not by nature. With the fall, they lost that gift of sanctifying grace through original sin, but God used the fall to bring about an even greater good.

God is so merciful that He used the fall of man to bring about his redemption, through the restoration of sanctifying grace *and* the elevation of human nature by the Incarnation of the Second Person of the Trinity. The angels were created higher than man in their *nature* (they have a superior intellect, they don't suffer, they are not constrained by space and time, etc.), but through the Incarnation, man has now been elevated higher than the angels by *grace*. It's amazing to think that God took His broken creature in the midst of his suffering and allowed him to fully share in the divine life of God. This is mercy!

God wants to show us what His mercy can do. He wants to show us that His mercy is greater than anything, even our sin. No, He didn't trump our free will and stop us from falling into sin, but He showed us His mercy by bringing us out of the misery of sin.

What's the worst evil in human history? Creatures nailing their very Creator to a Cross in a brutal execution. What is the greatest good in post-fallen human history? The salvation that came from that Cross. Our sinful action brought God's merciful response. O happy fault!

Suffering: What Is It Good for?

The fall had its lasting negative effects, however, which we call *concupiscence*. Defined as our innate selfishness and disordered drives resulting from original sin, concupiscence leads us to sin, causing a separation from God and a multitude of sufferings — physically, emotionally, and spiritually.

Taking all of this into consideration, we can see why we are destined to suffer in this life and why God allows it to happen. But let's not despair; rather, let's explore the *value* of suffering. We can learn a lot about the value of suffering from Scripture and from many saints and theologians.

Let's start with St. Faustina. Jesus told her, **"You will save more souls through prayers and suffering than will a missionary through his teachings and sermons alone"** (*Diary*, 1767). This means that all of you reading this potentially have more power to save souls than an ordained priest like me. Your sufferings have that much power!

Saint Faustina also wrote, "If the angels were capable of envy, they would envy us for two things: one is the receiving of Holy Communion, and the other is suffering" (*Diary*, 1804). The reason for this is that angels cannot physically suffer or receive Holy Communion because they are pure spirit. Thus, they would envy us because we most imitate Jesus when we suffer in the flesh as He did; it is then that we are most closely united to Him on the Cross. This is why St. Faustina wrote, "The Lord also gave me to understand what unimaginable glory awaits the person who resembles the suffering Jesus here on earth. That person will resemble Jesus in His glory" (*Diary*, 604).

I realize it is much easier to tell someone to accept their suffering than it is to accept it ourselves. It's easy for us to believe that no one fully understands our suffering, but it is important that we trust God does and believe that there are good reasons He allows it. In fact, we can trust that there really is value to our suffering.

Father Michael Shields, a Catholic priest in Anchorage, Alaska, in an article for the *North Star Catholic*, gives us a profound insight regarding the value of accepting our suffering:

> It is when we offer our suffering — the one thing most disagreeable to our human nature — back to God, the creator, that it becomes a gift of inestimable value, drawing down from Heaven more grace than any other action we can possibly make.[41]

When I first read this, I said to myself, "How can this be true? *Love* has the greatest power to draw down graces from Heaven." Then I read the next line of the article, a quote attributed to the great Jesuit priest and theologian Fr. John Hardon, SJ: "We love only to the degree that we are willing to suffer."[42] In other words, love and suffering are united. The article expanded on this theme: "We must never forget the defining moment of redemption for humanity was not when our Lord preached in the synagogues or healed the sick. It was when Love was nailed to a cross and drained of his blood. If love is willing to suffer, then love and suffering are inseparable."[43]

The Bible also tells us, "Greater love has no man than this, that a man lay down his life for his friends" (Jn 15:13, RSVCE). I like to say that there is no greater love than when someone suffers and dies to save their own executioners, which is what made Jesus' sacrifice so selfless and life-giving.

Redemption doesn't end, however, with Jesus' act of love. We too can take part in this incredible mystery of salvation even now. In his 1984 apostolic letter *Salvifici Doloris* (*On the Christian Meaning of Human Suffering*), John Paul II stated, "Each man, in his suffering, can also become a sharer in the redemptive suffering of Christ."[44] As Fr. George Kosicki, CSB, and Vinny Flynn explain it in their book *Now is the Time for Mercy*, "Christ sanctified suffering, making it salvific by His love. Now the Lord invites us to be partners in the work of salvation by bringing his mercy to everyone."[45]

I can hear some of you saying, "Wait a minute, Father, there's only one Redeemer: Jesus Christ. How can we be partners with Him?" It's true that Christ is the one and only Redeemer, but being a "partner" or "sharer" in Christ's redemptive suffering does not mean that we are on the same level as Christ. We are not equal to Christ the Redeemer, but we unite *with* Him in His redeeming act of Salvation. When we unite our sufferings with His on the Cross, we become partners with Him in His work of salvation.

The writings of St. Faustina amplify this point. Jesus told her, **"I thirst. I thirst for the salvation of souls. Help Me, My daughter, to save souls. Join your sufferings to My Passion and offer them to the heavenly Father for sinners"** (*Diary*, 1032). This means that we are to unite our sufferings to Christ's, not so we can be the source of grace, but so we can be instruments used by God to help souls receive His grace.

Saint Paul reiterated this point in Scripture when he wrote, "I am now rejoicing in my sufferings for your sake, and in my flesh I am completing what is lacking in Christ's afflictions for the sake of his body, that is, the church" (Col 1:24, RSVCE). If you're like me, you may ask, "What could possibly be lacking in the sufferings of Christ?" The answer: our sufferings.

So when you have a headache, when your children are driving you absolutely crazy, or whatever difficulties you may incur, you can offer up your crosses in union with Christ's Cross. Don't let a single moment of suffering go by without offering it up. Pray this prayer: "Lord, please accept my suffering in atonement for my sins and the sins of the whole world." In this way, you can actually help to save souls.

Blessed Dina Belanger taught us that if we understood the worth of our crosses, we would be rendered speechless with happiness and joy upon receiving them. (I'm not sure I am at this level of spirituality yet, but I'm trying.) Each morning and at every Mass, we should offer our sufferings along with Jesus to God the Father.

John Paul II underscored the importance of offering our sufferings to God when he wrote:

> It is precisely *the Church,* which ceaselessly draws on the infinite resources of the Redemption ... in which the redemptive suffering of Christ can be constantly completed by the suffering of man.[46]

That makes perfect sense, since it is in the Church that we unite our sufferings with the sufferings of Christ. This is the same point that St. Paul made about the value of suffering, and that is why your heartfelt participation at every Mass is so important. Don't just sit in the back of the Church during Mass looking at your watch. This is when you should offer your sufferings to Christ on the Cross, as we described in Chapter One.

The fact that we can help others through our sufferings emphasizes the divine and human nature of the Church. Father Kosicki and Vinny Flynn further highlight the important role our suffering plays in saving souls:

> The saving work of Jesus is not finished. He needs us to cooperate with His work of redemption and

bring His mercy to this generation. This kind of partnership involves a sharing in His sufferings in order to share in His saving work of mercy. This is the meaning of suffering. It is salvific, it is precious, don't waste it.[47]

Wow, the work of Christ isn't finished? That may seem shocking, especially to non-Catholics, but it shows the power God has given us in our suffering.

I often visit assisted-living centers to administer the Sacraments. When I do, I am often asked, "Father, what is the Church teaching on physician-assisted suicide?" And I always reply, "God bless you. But may I ask why you're asking?"

"Father, I'm just a burden. I'm a burden to my family. I'm draining them financially. I'm a burden to these beautiful staff members here. They have to take care of me all hours of the night. I offer nothing anymore to society. I'm nothing but a burden."

In response, I tell them emphatically, "Nothing could be further from the truth! One ounce of your suffering has more power than an atomic bomb, because united to the Cross of Christ, it can save souls. Do you ever lay in bed saying, 'I pray for the salvation of my son or my daughter,' or 'I really worry about the salvation of my husband or my wife?' You have an opportunity to make a difference in their destiny, not just yours, through your suffering!"

When we are ill and powerless to help ourselves, it can provide an opportunity for others to grow in compassion and practice the corporal works of mercy on our behalf. This is a precious gift for them. This can help sanctify their souls and lead them to eternal rewards (remember Matthew 25).

Remember, God did not intend for us just to be passive recipients of His grace. We are *active* participants in Christ's redemptive work. This is one of the big differences between the teachings of the Catholic Church and all other Christian religions.

God's Will Through the Cross

This does not mean that we should beg God to pile on unabated suffering in our life. Rather, we should do as Christ did during His Agony in the Garden, praying that the cup of suffering passes us by, but only if it is the will of God to take it away.

Redemptive suffering does not earn us forgiveness of sins (only Confession guarantees forgiveness), but it is another way (in addition to those we've already discussed) that can help reduce the punishment we are owed for our sins, such as the purification and detachment from earthly life that we will endure in Purgatory. In this way, suffering can actually be considered an extension of God's mercy, because the more we suffer, the more we can offer up to atone for our sins and the sins of others, possibly leading someone to salvation when they would have otherwise been lost.

Our Lord is so merciful that He allows us to remit some or *all* of the punishment due for our sins here on earth, instead of facing much worse punishment after death. Saints have said that one ounce of suffering in this life is worth more than a thousand pounds after we die. So as strange as it seems, the worst cross of all is to have no cross at all! Once again, our Lord is the Lord of paradox.

Jesus said to St. Faustina, **"[T]here is no way to heaven except the way of the cross. I followed it first. You must learn that it is the shortest and surest way"** (*Diary*, 1487).

The enemy will use our suffering and crosses to try to lead us to despair, but hold fast — we all have to go through these tests. By allowing us to be tested, God is showing us just how weak we are without Him or how strong we are when we entrust our difficulties to Him (one or the other, depending upon how we handle those difficulties).

If we pass this test, we will be perfected, and persever-ance in suffering is the best way to do this. Remember, God will not give us more than we can handle. When we take refuge in God, when we come to Him in trust and place our fears, our needs, our insecurities before Him, He makes our burdens easy and our crosses light.

We need to ask Him for the grace to persevere, for the grace to be able to carry our cross with His help. Saint Faustina asked for this grace from Jesus (see *Diary*, 1484) so she gives us the example of imploring God's grace to have the strength to endure what He gives us to carry.

Suffering Can Wake Us Up

Sometimes God allows us to be tested in extreme ways, because only in tragedy do some of us ever turn to Him. This is an important aspect of our Catholic faith. For instance, we all know stories of rock stars who led lives of decadence and had nothing to do with God until tragedy hit. It was only after life-changing crises such as accidents and self-degradation through drug and alcohol abuse that many of them turned to God for mercy.

The same has been true of famous athletes, such as Joe Theismann, a well-known quarterback for the Washington Redskins in the 1970s and '80s. In 1985, his right leg was snapped in half by Giants linebacker Lawrence Taylor on Monday Night Football. It ended his career and required extensive rehabilitation.

Later, in response to those who called it a tragedy, Theismann said that it was "actually a blessing," because being immobilized and bedridden for months caused him to reflect on his life.[48] He suddenly realized he had become too focused on himself and his career, and that he needed to change his life, to become more interested in other people and more serious about the gifts God had given to him. That tragic accident was the catalyst for his return to God and his faith. It changed his life.[49]

A quote commonly attributed to Archbishop Fulton J. Sheen goes like this: "Sometimes the only way the good Lord can get into some hearts is to break them."[50] A broken heart can be a means to break our self-centeredness and our expectation of always being the "receiver" rather than the "giver." We should love the God of consolations, not just the consolations of God. We shouldn't love Him only for the gifts He can give us, because He can easily take those away. Many times when He does, and our hearts are broken, we can find in our misery opportunity for growth in virtue.

We can see another example of this in a great saint who's an expert on suffering: Padre Pio (1887-1968). This Capuchin mystic received the stigmata (bearing the wounds of Christ) for many years before his death. Over the course of his life, he endured a great deal of sickness and suffering, including being beaten up by demons. In his writings, he addressed why God allows us to suffer. Simply put, sometimes suffering is the only way God can get our attention and sometimes our suffering is the very entry point into a deeper relationship with Him.

Padre Pio recalled that Jesus said to him, "How many times would you have abandoned me, my son, if I had not crucified you. Beneath the cross, one learns love, and I do not give this to everyone, but only to those souls who are dearest to me."[51]

Have you ever noticed how some people appear to have all the treasures of the world, but don't have the most important gift of all: faith? Everything seems so perfect in their life, but it really isn't. It seems when God gives us the great gift of faith, He also gives us another great gift called suffering. Thank you, Jesus (I think!)

There's an interesting story in this regard about St. Teresa of Avila (1515-1582). There are many versions of this account, but the most popular one tells of St. Teresa crossing a river on her horse one day and how she was nearly swept away. She complained to the Lord about her trials, to which Jesus responded, "Do not complain, daughter, for it is ever thus that I treat My friends." In reply, she said, "Ah, Lord, it is also on that account that Thou hast so few!" or as we would say it today, "If this is how you treat your friends, no wonder you have so few."[52]

If everything in our life was perfect, we'd probably think we don't need God. Picture it this way. Could you imagine if you woke up every morning, and your husband looked at you and said, "Dear, you're still the most beautiful thing I've ever seen in my life! Let me make you breakfast. You just stay in bed." And then your kids came running in and gave you a big hug and said, "Mom, we love you so much! We just did the laundry, we did the dishes, and we can't wait to go to Mass with you." And then you go to work and your boss says, "You know what? You are the best employee — you should be the manager. I'm going to step down and recommend you to take over." Then you come home, all the bills are paid, you have all the money you could ever need, you never get sick, and there is no suffering.

In this case, would you ever feel a desperate need for God? Maybe not, if you have fallen into a state of self-sufficiency and independence that neglects the proper worship of God and prayers of supplication. Even if we have these joys in our life and keep them properly ordered, we must never lose sight of the fact that they are only temporal. This world will end, and then all that will matter is the eternal, spiritual realm. To prepare for this, we absolutely need God — there is no other way. So it behooves us to begin to start to see our need for Him right now in our daily lives, especially in the midst of trial and tribulation.

This is why Sacred Scripture supplies us with many instances of bad things happening to good people. Some examples include the murder of Abel (Gen 4); the suffering of Job (Job 1:13-22; 2:10; 13:15; Jas 5:11); the suffering of Joseph (Gen 37:23-36; 39:1-23); the suffering of Paul

(2 Cor 11:22-30; 12:7-10); and of course all the sufferings of Christ throughout the Gospels.

To be a suffering servant is actually a vocation from God. If you are enduring much distress physically, spiritually, or emotionally, it could be possible that you are a suffering servant. While you should not automatically jump to the conclusion that just because you suffer it means you have a vocational calling from God (nor should you automatically believe that just because you suffer you are being punished by God), it is nonetheless something that you should discern with the guidance of a spiritual director and pray about. The reason this is important is because otherwise we may never see God's mercy in such situations.

Remember, we the Church are the Bride of Christ, and with that comes the need to be purified, which allows us to be most like Him. And suffering is one of the most effective ways to be purified. We see a dramatic example of this in an illuminating incident recorded in St. Faustina's *Diary*:

> Jesus was suddenly standing before me, stripped of His clothes, His body completely covered with wounds, His eyes flooded with tears and blood, His face disfigured and covered with spittle. The Lord then said to me, **The bride must resemble her Betrothed.** I understood these words to their very depth. There is no room for doubt here. My likeness to Jesus must be through suffering and humility (268).

Prayer and Suffering Can Get Us and Our Loved Ones to Heaven

Saint John Vianney (1786-1859), patron saint of priests and the wonder-working Curé d'Ars, was told during an exorcism that 80,000 souls had avoided hell because of his sanctity. This was surely because he prayed, endured suffering, and sacrificed heroically to save the souls of his parishioners.[53] That gives us some insight into the power of our suffering. If St. John Vianney could save 80,000 souls, then you can follow his example, and in even the smallest way give God your best effort to bear any crosses for the sake of souls.

The lives of the saints throughout the centuries provide numerous examples of prayer and redemptive suffering that you can look to for inspiration. Jesus told St. Faustina that the salvation of many souls depended on her prayers:

> **Pray as much as you can for the dying. By your entreaties, obtain for them trust in My mercy, because they have most need of trust, and have it the least. Be assured that the grace of eternal salvation for certain souls in their final moment depends on your prayer** (*Diary*, 1777).

Some people might misconstrue Jesus' words to mean that we have the same power as God. Of course, this is not the case, as only God can save souls. Remember, God simply uses us as instruments (in the words of John Paul II, we are "sharers" in Christ's work). He wants us to be participants in His work of salvation.

However, while all the grace for salvation comes from God, He can use us as channels to receive and transmit that grace. Jesus is the Head of the Body, and we are the members, carrying out His work, obeying His commands, and so helping to achieve His purpose. God is the *actual* cause of redemption, but we can be an *instrumental* cause.

When we choose to love as God loves, when we become instruments of His mercy, we can also avoid a huge pitfall, which we will discuss now.

Praise Him for Having Suffered More

At this point we should caution against focusing too much on our suffering, because even that can become prideful. We should avoid being overly concerned with proclaiming our struggles to others, instead finding time to lend an open ear to them. I often remind myself that I don't have to constantly broadcast my complaints to those around me; rather, I need to focus on the will of God and the needs of others as best I can. We should take an active interest in their sorrows and pains as well as our own and start praying for them as Jesus instructed St. Faustina to do. Like her, we will be responsible for praying for those souls God has entrusted to us.

One thing I've learned over the years is that no matter how difficult my sufferings have become, there is always someone who is undergoing more extreme trials than I am. Many times, after such insights, I have apologized to our Lord for my self-focus. Don't get me wrong: God wants to hear from us, and it is totally acceptable to complain to Him, as we read in the *Psalms of Lament* found in the Scriptures. But it is also important to be grateful for the blessings that God gives us even in the midst of our trials.

A helpful practice to implement when you begin to believe that your suffering has become overwhelming is to contemplate our Lord's walk to Calvary, meditating on what He endured during His bitter Passion. Thank Him for everything He has given you through His suffering and Passion, especially your salvation. Thank Him for paying your debt for sin so that you don't have to suffer eternally. Bless Him for dying for you so that you can have eternal life. When I do this, I get a new perspective on my worries, pains, and sufferings, and they no longer seem quite so bad. (Indeed, He makes our burdens easy and our crosses light.)

Did you know that saying "Blessed be God" once during periods of desolation is more powerful than saying it 100 times during periods of consolation? We grow most in difficult times, when we are pressed beyond our limit. Think about athletes who achieve greatness when their coaches push them beyond what they themselves think can they do.

The 1980 U.S. Olympic hockey team, which I mentioned in Chapter Four, was a classic example of this. They were a ragtag bunch of college kids who had never played professional hockey, while the Soviet national team was the greatest hockey team in the world. They had previously won several Olympic gold medals and even beat the NHL All-Stars quite handily in 1979. Ten days before the Olympics began, the American Olympic team was blown off the rink by this formidable Soviet squad in a pre-Olympics exhibition game.

The Americans were the underdogs of the entire competition and nobody gave them even the slightest chance of winning a medal, let alone the gold medal. That was until their coach, Herb Brooks, pushed them beyond what they thought was humanly possible. He challenged all hockey norms and called his players to a higher level, inspiring them to believe in themselves when no one else did. In a miraculous upset, named the greatest sporting event of the 20th century by *Sports Illustrated*, this American "David" slew the Soviet "Goliath" and went on to win the gold medal.

By pushing us beyond our limits, God helps us to grow. But we have a choice: We can accept our suffering and ask for God's mercy, like the good thief crucified next to Jesus who accepted his cross and asked Jesus to remember him, or we can be like the bad thief and reject our crosses (see Lk 23:39-43).

For Love of God and Neighbor

What we just read about on the importance of going beyond our limits and accepting our suffering is the starting point of something critical: *love*. Genuine love begins with self-sacrifice that enables us to transcend our natural limitations. Broken human nature tends toward selfishness and pleasure-seeking, the opposite of what we encounter in suffering. This is why we said earlier that suffering and love are inseparable.

Instead of self-centeredness, suffering teaches us true love, which is best exemplified in loving God and loving our neighbor. Interestingly, those just happen to be the two greatest commandments!

In her *Diary*, St. Faustina gives us an amazing insight into how suffering is inextricably linked to our love of God:

> [W]hen we suffer much we have a great chance to show God that we love Him; but when we suffer little we have less occasion to show God our love; and when we do not suffer at all, our love is then neither great nor pure. By the grace of God, we can attain a point where suffering will become a delight to us, for love can work such things in pure souls (303).

As we all know, there is nothing more important than loving God; in fact, our eternal fate depends on it. That makes this most unheralded of all reasons for accepting our suffering perhaps the most important of all. Through suffering, we can learn to love in a way that lasts eternally.

This is a powerful truth, because it tells us we can either accept suffering on this earth and enjoy eternity with God, or we can choose to enjoy our life here and suffer in eternity. I find this choice easy, and my prayer is *"Lord, please help me to accept my suffering here on earth; please cleanse me of my sins so that I can spend eternity with You in Heaven!"* Again, suffering is God's gift of mercy to us.

Similarly, suffering is also the paramount way to manifest our love of neighbor in that we can use our experiences to help someone else who is suffering presently. What better help might there be for a cancer patient than to be able to talk to a cancer survivor? Or for a mother who lost a child to suicide to be able to speak to a mother who now has to suddenly endure it? Saint Paul tells us, "Blessed be the God and Father of our Lord Jesus Christ, the Father of mercies and God of all comfort, who comforts us in all our affliction, so that we may be able to comfort those who are in any affliction, with the comfort with which we ourselves are comforted by God." (2 Cor 1:3-4, RSVCE).

Not only does this concept of love of neighbor apply to those for whom we offer our suffering, it also applies to those who cause us to suffer. Do you know who the saints tell us we will be most thankful for at the time of our death? *Annoying people.* And we all have them in our lives! Why? Without the crosses they provide, we would not be able to get to Heaven. Isn't that interesting?

Only at our judgment will we see how beneficial were these annoying people and all the trials they imposed upon us. They provide us with numerous opportunities to grow in patience and virtue. When we struggle with vices such as impatience, it shows that we still have a greater love of self than we do for our neighbor. Thus, the crosses imposed by others upon us can help us to grow in holiness and are part of God's plan for our salvation.

Suffering Summary

There are many reasons why God allows suffering. We can now summarize a few of the main points. The reasons include, but are not limited to the following:

- To diminish the appeal of this physical, temporal life. Heaven is what is important, not our brief existence on earth.

- To make us like His Son. Jesus suffered on the Cross, and we can be like Him.

- To purify our faith in God. It's purified by being tested, like gold in the fire (see 1 Pet 1:7).

- To teach us contentment and thankfulness; in other words, to accept what God gives us, the good and the bad. Job reminded us of this point.

- To teach us prayerfulness and dependence. When do most people turn back to God? When they get sick or a loved one is in danger. That is when they realize there is no one else who can help them.

- To perfect us in virtue.

- To help us develop compassion for others.

- To increase our love of God and neighbor.

- IT IS GOD'S MERCY!

Suffering is like a storm: Oftentimes it comes out of nowhere, ready to swamp our boat, and if we're not careful, we could even drown. But in every storm, Jesus is present, just as He was in the stories we read in the Gospels. He can remove the storm or at least get us through it, if we turn to Him in trust. The problem isn't the storm; the problem, as detailed in the beginning of this book, is our lack of trust.

Jesus told St. Faustina:

Know that your body and soul will often be in the midst of fire. Although you will not feel My presence on some occasions, I will always be with you. Do not fear; My grace will be with you (*Diary*, 1767).

When I think about suffering, I always return to the well-known poem "Footprints in the Sand." It is about a man looking back on his life, seeing it as though it were footprints on a beach. He sees that there are two sets of footprints for most of his life, and he knows that the other set of footprints show God walking beside him. Then he sees that at the hardest times in his life, there's only one set of footprints. He questions God, asking why, when he needed divine assistance most, God would ever leave him to walk on his own. God explains to the man that the single set of footprints are not those of the man, but of God, who carried the man through the hardest times.[54]

If we trust God, we know that He is closest to us in the times when everything seems darkest, when He seems furthest away or even absent entirely. But we can know that He is never absent, because if God ever truly left us alone, we'd cease to exist. So long as we are breathing and able to ask whether or not God loves us, the answer is that *He does love us.* He loved us into life, and He sustains our existence through His love and mercy.

I'm not expecting everyone to fully understand this when they are in the midst of extreme trauma or unrest. It is easy for someone to proclaim this doctrine when they're not in pain, when they're not the one struggling. But ultimately we can believe it thanks to the virtue of hope. Scripture gives us hope by telling us that in Heaven, God will wipe away all our tears (see Rev 21:3-4). We just have to get through this valley of tears, because "eye has not seen, and ear has not heard … what God has prepared for those who love him" (1 Cor 2:9, NABRE).

God's Mercy Is Present, Even After Tragedies

At some point in our lives, we will all experience tragedy or loss, whether it is in the form of sickness, disease, financial problems, or death. One such example is suicide. It's one of the most difficult of all tragedies to deal with, because we always feel that if we would have done something differently (or not done something), then our loved one would still be with us. The thought of suicide makes us cringe, and often we don't know how to talk about it.

The following story can be found in its entirety in my book *After Suicide: There's Hope for Them and for You*, coauthored with Br. Jason Lewis, MIC. However, the teaching and principles discussed therein apply not just to suicide, but to any kind of tragedy or loss. By telling this personal story of loss in my own life, I hope to convey the power of God's mercy.

As detailed in that book, I lost my grandmother to suicide. After many years of suffering from physical and emotional setbacks, she finally succumbed and "gave up the fight," tragically taking her own life in 1993. This event sent shockwaves through our entire family. Afterwards, we found her suicide very difficult to talk about, because as Catholics we had always been told that souls who take their own life will be eternally lost after death. It was for this reason that we never discussed my grandmother for 10 years following her death. It was almost as if we all wanted to erase this hurtful memory of our family's past — not the memory of her life, but the shock of her death.

Then in the early 2000s, I started to return to my Catholic faith after many years of being lukewarm at best. I never rejected my faith, but I hadn't been embracing it either, and I didn't practice it in any way other than a few Sunday and holiday Masses each year. This all changed, however, after moving to North Carolina to start my own business. Amidst the fire of faith found in the South, I experienced a string of "God events" in my life that fostered in me a new and incessant desire to pray, attend Mass, and read every devotional book I could get my hands on.

During this "reversion," I went to a General Confession in 2003 to lift some of the weight that had been on my shoulders from the past 20 years of sin since my last

Confession. One of the things I mentioned to the priest during that conversation was the feeling of guilt that I had carried after the death of my grandmother.

I lamented to him that I didn't even remember praying for her at her own funeral. Tortured by this sin of omission, I regretted that she needed my prayers when she was still alive and suffering so badly, but I was not there for her. This torment followed me for years after her death, because it was too late to help her — I believed that her soul was lost. When I told the priest that I had always believed Church teaching to be that if you take your own life, you are damned to hell, he set me straight. "No," he said, "that is not Church teaching." He educated me on several aspects of the Church's teaching on suicide and sin that I didn't know at the time, which I would like to briefly share here.

The reason many Catholics are told this is because early theologians considered suicide as self-murder, and therefore a mortal sin. Yes, objectively, suicide is grave matter (so is helping someone to take their own life). Please don't be swayed by people who say that assisted suicide is "mercy killing." There is no such thing as mercy killing, as Catholic teaching stresses that only God can determine when a soul is called from this earth.

We have to allow God's will to be done in such cases, even when suffering is involved, because God's mercy may be allowing a soul to go through purification and atonement in order to be saved. It is natural to want to completely relieve a person's suffering, but since that suffering may be for the salvation of their soul, or someone else's soul, it is not up to us to make the decision to curtail their life.

Suicide is considered grave matter because it is a sin against God and neighbor. God gave us life, and since only He determines when it ends, to take our own life is the sin of taking something that rightfully belongs to God. Suicide is also a sin against your neighbor because of all the pain it will cause your loved ones, which makes it the opposite of charity.

These early theologians also thought suicide to be damnable because it allows no time to repent; therefore, they believed the soul that takes its life is condemned because it dies in an unrepentant state of mortal sin. In light of this understanding, does the Church *still* teach that those who take their life automatically go to hell? Not necessarily. Although this sin could result in a soul being lost, the Church has never taught that any particular soul, even after suicide, is in hell.

Thus, while suicide is objectively grave matter, there is more to the story. As we just mentioned, there is only one way for a soul to be eternally lost and that is if the person dies in an unrepentant state of mortal sin. But for a sin to be mortal, three conditions must be present. First, the sin must be grave (serious) matter. Suicide is grave matter, as is violence done to another, sexual sin, or missing Mass on Sunday without reason, among other sins. Second, the person must have full knowledge that the act is a sin. Most people would acknowledge that suicide is a sin. Third, the person must fully intend to commit the act with complete free will. Let's talk about that for a moment.

This third condition is where things are not so "black and white." In the case of suicide, a person may not have full free will; they may not really want to take their own life. My grandma is an example of this. She struggled and tried everything just to get through another day. The suffering she was enduring was very difficult for her and she couldn't continue the fight, a fight that was wearing her down beyond her physical and emotional capabilities to endure it. As a result of this possible lack of free will, *subjectively speaking*, suicide may not be a mortal sin in the sense that in certain circumstances the person may not be fully culpable for their actions, as we will soon see.

My Grandmother's Suicide

I told the priest in North Carolina that on Father's Day, 1993, my grandmother made the tragic decision to take her own life. Using a handgun my grandfather bought her for protection against unwarranted fears of burglary, she clearly made the wrong choice. Suicide is never the right choice — it is a permanent response to temporary problems, no matter how serious those problems may be.

That being said, we must empathize with those who have succumbed and given up the fight. Due to their circumstances, these persons may not be guilty of despair in the sense that they have abandoned all trust in God and deliberately chosen to reject His mercy, thinking there is no hope for their salvation. Many suicide victims don't necessarily believe that God doesn't love them and doesn't want to save them. I know my grandmother didn't.

Often, these persons simply want their pain to end. They don't want to reject or offend God, or to commit a grave sin. They may have reached out for help with their mental or physical illness or emotional suffering, but to no avail. Does this make them guilty of a damnable sin? Again, not necessarily. The *Catechism* states, "Grave psychological disturbances, anguish, or grave fear of hardship, suffering, or torture can diminish the responsibility of the one committing suicide" (2282).

Over the years, the Church has transitioned away from a view of suicide based solely on the objective gravity of the sin, toward a more subjective view that considers the factors that lessen a person's culpability. Holy Mother Church has become more pastoral when dealing with such tragedies, regarding both the families involved and the deceased person in particular.

Subjectively, there may be mitigating factors such as mental illness or lack of free will that factor into a person's decision to take their own life, so no one can fully appreciate the unimaginable pain that causes such a tragedy. No one, therefore, can judge a person whose choice we cannot fathom. This is how the Church tends to look upon suicide today — pastorally and with pity, not condemnation.

The Church now understands that contemplating or completing suicide is a *misery*, and God's answer to misery has always been *mercy*. Father William Byron, SJ, once wrote:

> The Church still teaches that there is a hell, but leaves it to God to decide who should go there. And divine decisions, in this regard, are filtered through divine mercy. Tragedy at the end of this life is no sure sign of an eternal tragedy in the next.[55]

Let's return now to my General Confession in 2003. After listening to the priest educate me on Church teaching, I started to have hope for the possibility of my grandma's salvation. However, it still weighed heavily on my heart that I didn't pray for her at her funeral. In fact, this was a big reason I went to Confession in the first place.

I told the priest that instead of begging God's mercy on her soul at the time of her death, I was too busy worrying about the reputation of our family. I was preoccupied with our good name, trying to keep the fact that she took her life out of her obituary and away from public knowledge. It was a selfish act on my behalf, as I was more concerned with what people thought about her death than I was with what they thought about her life. My lack of concern at the time for her salvation had come to haunt me in the years after her funeral (although I was rather uneducated in Church teaching at the time of her death and perhaps not fully culpable).

Even 10 years after her death, I still carried much guilt about failing to pray for my grandma back in 1993. I then realized that I should have prayed for her right before her death, when I knew she was suffering. I also felt guilty that

I didn't pray for her right after she died, when I should have been praying for her as well.

I explained my concerns to the priest, and while I had some renewed hope based on what he said earlier, I thought it was still probable that my grandma's soul was in hell. To make matters worse, I believed that this was partly because I didn't pray for her or help her in any way when I had the opportunity. This bothered me to the core of my being and caused me great unrest. But what the priest said next changed the course of my entire life.

God Is Outside of Time

After explaining the whole story to my confessor, he told me, "Go home tonight and pray the Chaplet of Divine Mercy for the salvation of your grandmother's soul." I replied, "What is the Chaplet of Divine Mercy? I've never heard of it."

He responded, "I'll teach you how to pray it in a minute. It's a simple prayer and it's one of the most powerful prayers you could ever make in your life, outside of the Mass."

"But Father," I said, "my grandmother died 10 years ago, how can any prayers I say now help her with her salvation after she has already been judged? She is either in Heaven or in hell; the fact is she has been judged, so her eternal fate is sealed — whatever that fate may be. At best, all my prayers might be able to do is relieve some of her time in Purgatory, if she even made it that far."

He said, "Look, God is outside of time. There is no time for God; there is no past, there is no future. For God everything happens at once. Everything occurs in one, great big 'eternal present moment' for God. In other words, God sees everything that has ever happened or will ever happen instantaneously."

The priest continued, "God is *omniscient*, meaning He is all-knowing. He knows every prayer you will ever make in your entire life. He is also *omnipotent*, meaning He is all-powerful. He has the power to apply the graces from the prayers you make to any point in time — past, present, or future. So go home tonight and pray the Chaplet to help your grandma at the moment of her judgment."

While completely captivated with this new information about the nature of God, I was still unsure of how to process everything that was going on in my mind. Seeing this, the priest gave an illustrative example. He referred to a saint I was familiar with, St. Padre Pio.

The priest pointed to the fact that there exists documentation of an interesting story about Padre Pio from Fr. Alessio Parente, OFM Cap, Padre Pio's personal assistant. Parente recounts the following conversation between Padre Pio and his physician:

> Padre Pio: "[I] can pray even now for the happy death of my great-grandfather."
>
> Doctor: "But he has been dead for many, many years."
>
> Padre Pio: "For the Lord, the past doesn't exist; the future doesn't exist. Everything is an eternal present. Those prayers had already been taken into account. And so I repeat that even now I can pray for the happy death of my great-grandfather!"[56]

After hearing this, I exclaimed, "You mean I can get her out of hell?"

"No!" he answered. "That's not Church teaching. But your prayers even now can actually assist her at the moment of her judgment." He continued, "Jesus told St. Faustina in her *Diary*..."

I interrupted him, asking, "Who is St. Faustina and what is the *Diary*?"

He explained who she was and the mission Jesus gave her (see Chapter Two), and then he resumed his main point: "Jesus told St. Faustina that He comes to the soul three times at the moment of death, giving the person three opportunities to accept His mercy (see *Diary*, 1486). In a particular example she records in the *Diary*, Jesus comes to a despairing soul, pleading with the soul to accept His gift of salvation."

Excited, I shouted, "Father! Then we are done here! Because there is no way Jesus is going to come to my grandmother without her jumping into His arms and saying, 'point the elevator up, let's go!'"

Bringing me back down to reality, he softly responded, "No so fast. Did your grandmother receive the Sacraments before she died?

"I don't know."

"Did she reconcile with God and ask for His forgiveness and mercy?" He asked.

Again I replied, "I don't know."

"The problem is we die in the state that we live, and if your grandmother turned her back on God in this life, she may not recognize Christ when He comes to her at the moment of her death."

"What?" I said. "Father, you had me optimistic for her salvation, now you are telling me she won't recognize Jesus when He comes?"

"You didn't let me finish," he retorted. "*Without* your prayers, she may not recognize Him when He comes. But *with* your prayers, the veil that is blocking her vision of God, her sin so to speak, can be lifted with the grace of your prayers, and she can see God for who He is."

"Wow," was the only word that I could muster.

The priest continued, "She is going to really need your help. So, as I said, go home tonight and pray the Chaplet of Divine Mercy for the salvation of your grandmother's soul!"

The priest compared the graces from my prayers to a squadron of dive bombers, flying in from 2003 back to 1993, to the moment of my grandma's judgment, through the hands of our Blessed Mother, and showered upon her soul. The priest said that God would allow the grace of my prayers to be given to her because prayers have that kind of power. They could help to lift the veil from her eyes, increasing her ability to say "yes" to God and accept His mercy, when otherwise she may not have "recognized" Jesus when He came for her.

Remember, Jesus comes for us when we enter into eternity, on the eighth day. That is why, as we explained in Chapter Three, we need to be ready! That is the most guaranteed and surest way of salvation, but even if the soul of our loved one is not perfectly prepared, we can still have hope through our prayers. Of course, we need to understand that we can't make the decision for our loved ones and say "yes" to God for them. Only they can accept Christ at the moment of their judgment, but the graces from our prayers can definitely aid them in doing so.

As mentioned earlier, God wants us to participate in His saving act of redemption, which is why Jesus told St. Faustina that the salvation of thousands of souls depended on her prayers. This can also be seen in the apparitions at Fatima, when the Blessed Virgin Mary said, "Pray, pray very much. Make sacrifices for sinners. Many souls go to hell, because no one is willing to help them with sacrifice."[57]

Our prayers and sufferings united to Christ matter more than we can imagine, and God can accomplish more with that grace than we can ever know in this life.

No Time to Repent?

Almost sold on this most incredible concept, I still had one last objection. Thinking in line with those early Church theologians, I hesitantly asked, "Father, my grandma shot herself with a handgun and died instantly. There was no time to repent. Doesn't that affect things?"

Frustrated in a loving way, he said, "Nothing is outside the mercy of God! Remember, Jesus comes to the soul and gives them the opportunity to receive His mercy."

The priest was concerned for me because he understood what I and so many others have gone through. Whether a person dies by suicide or by any other means, loved ones of the deceased often worry that the person didn't have time before they died to "make things right with God." They are concerned that their loved one may not have had time to repent of their sins and ask for God's mercy. The Church weighs in on this matter, especially regarding suicide (and we can have hope that God's mercy extends to all unprepared deaths).

To help me understand this, the priest then read to me from the *Catechism*:

> We should not despair of the eternal salvation of persons who have taken their own lives. By ways known to him alone, God can provide the opportunity for salutary repentance. The Church prays for persons who have taken their own lives (2283).

Amazed, I begged him to elaborate. He said to me in reply, "You don't think that in the time it took that bullet to travel three inches, God can't work a miracle? In that microsecond between her decision to pull the trigger and her death, God can come to the soul, even three times. This is possible because God is not constrained by time."

Then he let me know there was even more support for what he was telling me. He read this passage from the *Diary* of St. Faustina:

> God's mercy sometimes touches the sinner at the last moment in a wondrous and mysterious way. Outwardly, it seems as if everything were lost, but it is not so. The soul, illumined by a ray of God's powerful final grace, turns to God in the last moment with such a power of love that, in

an instant, it receives from God forgiveness of sin and punishment, while outwardly it shows no sign either of repentance or of contrition, because souls at that stage no longer react to external things. Oh, how beyond comprehension is God's mercy! ... Although a person is at the point of death, the merciful God gives the soul that interior vivid moment, so that if the soul is willing, it has the possibility of returning to God (1698).

This revelation of God's mercy, together with the words from the *Catechism* on hope for those who have taken their own lives, tell us how God offers the opportunity for repentance from our sins, no matter how grave.

Concluding the most incredible conversation I ever had in my life, I shouted, "Are you kidding me? We have a God so loving, so merciful, that He would allow a knucklehead like me, who didn't even pray for his grandma at her funeral, to have an opportunity years later to aid in the salvation of her soul? And then He will shower graces from those prayers on her soul at the moment of her death, giving her the opportunity to repent and be saved? That's absolutely incredible!"

My Life Changes

At that point, I said to the priest, "Father, I don't know how, but I have to spend the rest of my life spreading this message of God's mercy! This is beyond anything I had ever heard!" Of course, I had no idea that God would make me a priest, but this is how He works.

The priest then handed me a prayer card bearing the Image of Divine Mercy, Jesus Christ, on the front, and on the back were instructions on how to pray the Chaplet of Divine Mercy. He told me that this was the most powerful prayer, along with the Rosary, that we can make outside of the Mass. And take a guess where that prayer card was from? The Association of Marian Helpers in Stockbridge, Massachusetts! And guess who is now the director of the Association of Marian Helpers? You guessed it, I am. Once again, this is how God's mercy works!

I was so moved by how merciful God is, that it changed my entire life. I went home that night and prayed the Chaplet of Divine Mercy for the salvation of my grandmother's soul, and I definitely felt a certain peace afterwards and a sense that she was allowed entry into Heaven. So when you say this prayer, have that same kind of trust. That's why I joined the Marian Fathers of the Immaculate Conception of the Most Blessed Virgin Mary. We are the Divine Mercy priests and this is the message we are tasked to spread around the world.

There is one last story that I wish to share. It is about what we should do when doubt tries to undermine our trust in God's mercy. As a Marian priest, I have spoken at many parish missions. During one of those missions a couple of years ago, I began to doubt whether the story of my grandma and the power of prayer was really true. I began to doubt if I should even continue to tell the story at my mission talks, but at least I prayed and tried to discern what to do. I told God in prayer that I wasn't going to continue to include the story anymore in my talks unless He gave me some sort of assurance that it was His will. I wasn't challenging God; I just didn't want to be teaching something if it wasn't true.

It took all of three hours for God to answer. As I was walking across the parking lot, heading to the church for the final night of my mission, I was convincing myself not to tell this story. Halfway there, I noticed a young lady getting out of her car. Our eyes briefly made contact, and then she asked, "Are you Fr. Joseph?" I told her that was my honorary title as the director of the Association of Marian Helpers, but I introduced myself as Fr. Chris. She continued, "Do you have a minute to talk?" When I told her I did, she inquired, "Are you the one who made the DVD about your grandmother taking her life?"

"Yes, I am," I told her.

"I have to talk to you, Father," she said. "My uncle took his own life, and like you, I didn't pray for him. And for years, I thought he was in hell. Then I watched your DVD and started praying the Chaplet for him. Again, like you, I felt something. Then one day I went to Confession to a very holy priest who is known for being able to read souls. After my Confession, during which I hadn't mentioned my uncle at all, the priest said, 'By the way, your Chaplets worked.' I said, 'What do you mean, Father?' And he replied, 'Didn't you have an uncle who took his life and you were praying the Chaplet of Divine Mercy for him? Your Chaplets worked.' I asked him, 'How did you know about that when I didn't mention him in my Confession?' And he said, 'I just saw it.'"

A chill went down my spine and I proceeded directly into the church that night and told this story, emphasizing to never doubt the mercy of God. God can bring a greater good out of even the worst tragedy, and He never wants evil to have the last word. I truly believe that the greater good that came from my grandma's unfortunate situation was my priesthood. I also believe that my prayers aided her in accepting God's mercy at the moment of her judgment, when Jesus offered her eternal salvation. This is how the Body of Christ works.

God's mercy is always with us and is greater than any sin, even suicide. Divine Mercy is an ocean, next to which any sin, no matter how grave, is a mere drop. All sins are forgivable except one: refusing to accept God's mercy. In other words, all we have to do is ask for it. This is the key — remember your ABCs!

Our faith offers us endless ways to invite the grace of God into our lives and into any painful situation. Divine Mercy is always the answer. We are called to imitate the example of the early Church: In the face of the persecution that came, the disciples could have lost hope. But Jesus had told them — and demonstrated in His own life — that we must go through the Crucifixion before we experience the Resurrection.

This means that we have hope, real hope, supernatural hope coming from God Himself, not just in response to suicide but to all tragedies, for healing through God's mercy. No tragedy, no matter how bad, is beyond God's mercy. He is always with us, helping us get through it. As a great friend of mine, Sammie Wood once said, "You will never get *over* such devastating events in your life, but with the mercy of God you can get *through* them."

That is what Divine Mercy is, and what it can do for us is truly incredible. It is so incredible, in fact, that it can change your life now, and for all eternity. That is why it is absolutely necessary for you to receive Divine Mercy — and we have the words of Jesus to confirm that: **"I am giving mankind the last hope of salvation; that is, recourse to My mercy"** (*Diary*, 998).

How to Pray the Chaplet of Divine Mercy

1. Make the Sign of the Cross.

2. Say the optional Opening Prayer.

3. Say the "Our Father."

4. Say the "Hail Mary."

5. Say the "Apostles' Creed."

6. Say the "Eternal Father."

7. Say 10 "For the sake of His sorrowful Passion" on the "Hail Mary" beads.

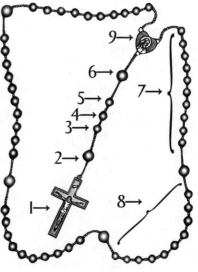

8. Repeat for four more decades, saying "Eternal Father" on the "Our Father" bead and then 10 "For the Sake of His sorrowful Passion" on the following "Hail Mary" beads.

9. At the conclusion of the five decades, on the medallion say the "Holy God," the concluding doxology, three times.

10. Say the optional Closing Prayer.

Prayers of the Chaplet of Divine Mercy

1. *The Sign of the Cross:* In the name of the Father, and of the Son, and of the Holy Spirit. Amen.

2. *Opening Prayers (optional):* You expired, Jesus, but the source of life gushed forth for souls, and the ocean of mercy opened up for the whole world. O Fount of Life, unfathomable Divine Mercy, envelop the whole world and empty Yourself out upon us (*Diary*, 1319).

   O Blood and Water, which gushed forth from the Heart of Jesus as a fount of mercy for us, I trust in You! (*three times*) (*Diary*, 84).

3. *The Our Father:* Our Father, who art in heaven; hallowed be Thy name; Thy kingdom come; Thy will be done on earth as it is in heaven. Give us this day our daily bread; and forgive us our trespasses as we forgive those who trespass against us, and lead us not into temptation; but deliver us from evil. Amen.

4. *The Hail Mary:* Hail Mary, full of grace. The Lord is with thee. Blessed art thou among women, and blessed is the fruit of thy womb, Jesus. Holy Mary, Mother of God, pray for us sinners, now and at the hour of our death. Amen.

5. *The Apostles' Creed:* I believe in God, the Father almighty, Creator of Heaven and earth, and in Jesus Christ, His only Son, our Lord, who was conceived by the Holy Spirit, born of the Virgin Mary, suffered under Pontius Pilate, was crucified, died, and was buried; He descended into hell; on the third day He rose again from the dead; He ascended into Heaven, and is seated at the right hand of God the Father almighty; from there He will come to judge the living and the dead. I believe in

the Holy Spirit, the holy catholic Church, the Communion of saints, the forgiveness of sins, the resurrection of the body, and life everlasting. Amen.*

6. *On the "Our Father" bead before each decade:* Eternal Father, I offer You the Body and Blood, Soul and Divinity of Your dearly beloved Son, Our Lord Jesus Christ, in atonement for our sins and those of the whole world (*Diary*, 476).

7. *On the "Hail Mary" beads of each decade:* For the sake of His sorrowful Passion, have mercy on us and on the whole world.

8. *Repeat "Eternal Father" and "For the Sake of His sorrowful Passion":* (Number 6 and 7) Prayers for four more decades.

9. *After five decades, the concluding doxology (three times):* Holy God, Holy Mighty One, Holy Immortal One, have mercy on us and on the whole world.

10. *Closing Prayer (optional):* Eternal God, in whom mercy is endless, and the treasury of compassion inexhaustible, look kindly upon us, and increase Your mercy in us, that in difficult moments, we might not despair, nor become despondent, but with great confidence, submit ourselves to Your holy will, which is Love and Mercy Itself. Amen (*Diary*, 950).

*The wording of the Apostles' Creed conforms with the Roman Missal.

Endnotes

[1] *Konferencja ascetyczne. Notatki sguchaczy przemówien Ojca Maksymiliana Kolbego (Ascetical Conferences of Father Maximilian Kolbe from the Notes of Those Who Heard Him)*, Niepokalanow, 1976, March 10, 1940, quoted in "St. Maximilian Kolbe and the Eucharist," Mother of All Peoples, updated May 29, 2020, https://www.motherofallpeoples.com/post/st-maximilian-kolbe-and-the-eucharist.

[2] St. Thomas Aquinas, *Summa Theologiae* I, 10, 1.

[3] Joseph Cardinal Ratzinger, *The Spirit of the Liturgy*, trans. John Saward (San Francisco: Ignatius Press, 2014), pp. 70-71.

[4] Ibid., pp. 57, 60.

[5] "Man, tempted by the devil, let his trust in his Creator die in his heart and, abusing his freedom, disobeyed God's command. This is what man's first sin consisted of. All subsequent sin would be disobedience toward God and lack of trust in his goodness." English translation of the *Catechism of the Catholic Church* (Washington, DC/Vatican: United States Catholic Conference, Inc./Libreria Editrice Vaticana, 1997), n. 397.

[6] It may appear as if I'm saying that only the Father creates, only the Son redeems, and only the Spirit sanctifies/divinizes. But where any one Person of the Trinity is, there are the other two. This presentation is simply based on which Person of the Trinity is most associated with particular portions of salvation history, not some rigid division of their roles.

[7] Pope Benedict XVI, *Regina Cæli, Angelus* message, March 30, 2008, http://www.vatican.va/content/benedict-xvi/en/angelus/2008/documents/hf_ben-xvi_reg_20080330.html.

[8] Pope St. John Paul II, Encyclical Letter *Dives in Misericordia (Rich in Mercy)*, November 30, 2008, n. 7, http://www.vatican.va/content/john-paul-ii/en/encyclicals/documents/hf_jp-ii_enc_30111980_dives-in-misericordia.html.

[9] Robert Fulghum, *All I Really Need to Know I Learned in Kindergarten* (New York: Villard Books, 1986).

[10] Pope St. John Paul II, Address, Shrine of Divine Mercy, Krakow, Poland, June 7, 1997, n. 1, http://www.vatican.va/content/john-paul-ii/en/speeches/1997/june/documents/hf_jp-ii_spe_19970607_divina-misericordia.html.

[11] Fr. Paul Yi, "Trust: A Journey into the Diary of St. Faustina, Talk 1," Homilies of Father Paul Yi, June 17, 2015, Ascension Catholic Church, Donaldsonville, LA, reproduced at http://jesusthrumary.blogspot.com/2015/06/trust-journey-through-diary-of-st.html.

[12] Sr. Madeleine Grace, CVI, "Sr. Faustina Kowalska: A Model for Eucharistic Spirituality," *Homiletic & Pastoral Review* (San Francisco, CA: Ignatius Press, April 2008), pp. 68 – 73.

[13] Ewa Czaczkowska, *Faustina: The Mystic and Her Message* (Stockbridge, MA: Marian Press, 2014), pp. 340, 358.

[14] See, for example, Czaczkowska, pp. 372-73.

[15] Fr. Paul Yi, "Trust: A Journey into the Diary of St. Faustina, Talk 1," June 17, 2015, Ascension Catholic Church, Donaldsonville, LA, reproduced at http://jesusthrumary.blogspot.com/2015/06/trust-journey-through-diary-of-st.html.

[16] Taken from "Session One: God's School of Trust," in Divine Mercy in the Second Greatest Story Ever Told, DVD, (Greenwood Village, CO: Augustine Institute Studios, 2016).

[17] Fr. Thaddaeus Lancton, MIC, *Stepping on the Serpent: The Journey of Trust with Mary* (Stockbridge, MA: Marian Press, 2017).

[18] Blessed Sebastian Valfre, quoted in Jill Haak Adels, *The Wisdom of the Saints: An Anthology* (New York: Oxford University Press, 1989), p. 64.

[19] Blessed Francis Xavier Seelos, quoted in "Saint of the Day: Blessed Francis Xavier Seelos, 'The Cheerful Ascetic,'" *Aleteia*, accessed December 20, 2020, https://aleteia.org/daily-prayer/friday-october-5/.

[20] Fernand Cabrol, "Octave," in *The Catholic Encylopedia* (New York: Robert Appleton Company, 1911), New Advent, https://www.newadvent.org/cathen/11204a.htm.

[21] Yehushuah Stokar, "The Magical Number of 8," Torah Mitzion, June 7, 2015, https://torahmitzion.org/learn/the-magical-number-of-8/.

[22] Eliezer Posner, "What is the Spiritual Significance of the Number Eight?" Chabad.org, accessed November 20, 2020, https://www.chabad.org/library/article_cdo/aid/606168/jewish/Whats-the-Significance-of-the-Number-Eight.htm.

[23] TheDivineMercy.org, "Image, Feast, and a New Millennium of Mercy!" July 28, 2006, https://www.thedivinemercy.org/articles/image-feast-and-new-millenium-mercy.

[24] Apostolic Penitentiary, *Manual of Indulgences* (USCCB, 2006), Other Concessions, Introduction, 7.

[25] Note that the *Catechism* (1452) states that an Act of Contrition still requires sacramental Confession to receive forgiveness of mortal sins: "When it arises from a love by which God is loved above all else, contrition is called 'perfect' (contrition of charity). Such contrition remits venial sins; it also obtains forgiveness of mortal sins if it includes the firm resolution to have recourse to sacramental Confession as soon as possible." A standard Act of Spiritual Communion is as follows:

> My Jesus,
> I believe that You are present in the Blessed Sacrament.
> I love You above all things,
> and I desire to receive You into my soul.
> Since I cannot at this moment receive You sacramentally,
> come at least spiritually into my heart.
> I embrace You as if You were already there
> and unite myself wholly to You.
> Never permit me to be separated from You.
> Amen.

[26] Ewa Czaczkowska, *Faustina: The Mystic and Her Message* (Stockbridge, MA: Marian Press, 2014), p. 22.

[27] Author conversation with Fr. Seraphim Michalenko, MIC, December 18, 2020.

[28] Father Johann G. Roten, SM, "Modern Apparitions, New Forms: A New Type of Apparition," University of Dayton: All About Mary, https://udayton.edu/imri/mary/m/modern-apparitions-new-forms.php.

[29] Ratzinger, *Spirit of the Liturgy*, pp. 132-33.

[30] Robert Bucklin, "The Shroud of Turin: Viewpoint of a Forensic Pathologist*," *Shroud Spectrum International* 5, part 3 (December 1982), pp. 3-10, https://www.shroud.com/pdfs/ssi05part3.pdf.

[31] "God made me to know Him, to love Him, and to serve Him in this world, and to be happy with Him forever in the next." Third Plenary Council of Balti-

more, *Baltimore Catechism No. Two* (Charlotte, NC: TAN Books, 2010), Lesson First, "On the End of Man," Question 6, p. 8.

[32] See, for instance, St. John Damascene's Apologetic Treatises against those Decrying the Holy Images.

[33] Quote drawn from the first booklet Fr. Sopocko ever published on the Divine Mercy message and devotion, printed in Krakow during St. Faustina's lifetime.

[34] Ibid.

[35] The *Summarium of the Cause of the Beatification and Canonization of Faustina Kowalska of the Congregation of Sisters of the Blessed Virgin Mary of Mercy,* from Session XVI, December 14, 1965 (public copy).

[36] Vatican II, *Apostolicam Actuositatem (Decree on the Apostolate of the Laity)*, November 18, 1965, http://www.vatican.va/archive/hist_councils/ii_vatican_council/documents/vat-ii_decree_19651118_apostolicam-actuositatem_en.html, n. 2.

[37] "[I]t was between the First and Second World Wars that Christ entrusted his message of mercy to her. Those who remember, who were witnesses and participants in the events of those years and the horrible sufferings they caused for millions of people, know well how necessary was the message of mercy. ... Sr Faustina's canonization has a particular eloquence: by this act I intend today to pass this message on to the new millennium. I pass it on to all people, so that they will learn to know ever better the true face of God and the true face of their brethren." Pope St. John Paul II, Homily, April 30, 2000, http://www.vatican.va/content/john-paul-ii/en/homilies/2000/documents/hf_jp-ii_hom_20000430_faustina.html. See also Michael Gaitley, *The Second Greatest Story Ever Told: Now is the Time of Mercy* (Stockbridge, MA: Marian Press, 2015).

[38] Pope St. John Paul II, Address, Shrine of Divine Mercy, Krakow, Poland, June 7, 1997, n. 1, http://www.vatican.va/content/john-paul-ii/en/travels/1997/documents/hf_jp-ii_spe_07061997_sr-faustina.html.

[39] Pope Benedict XVI, *Regina Cæli, Angelus* message, April 23, 2006, http://www.vatican.va/content/benedict-xvi/en/angelus/2006/documents/hf_ben-xvi_reg_20060423.html.

[40] "Father Seraphim located Dr. Valentin Fuster, a world-renowned cardiologist, to review the case. His testimony advanced the case quickly with Fr. Seraphim working with Vatican officials on the needed documentation. So, on Divine Mercy Sunday, April 30, 2000, Pope John Paul II canonized St. Faustina in Rome as the first saint of the Great Jubilee Year 2000. Father Seraphim, Fr. Pytel, and Dr. Fuster were all present for the big day. John Paul II even attended the reception after the canonization. He told Dr. Fuster, 'This is the happiest day of my life.'" "Last Will and Testament of Mercy," *Marian Helper* (Summer 2005), https://www.thedivinemercy.org/articles/last-will-and-testament-mercy.

[41] Fr. Michael Shields, "Let Me Suffer and Love with You Lord. Only with You," *North Star Catholic,* February 2019, https://northstarcatholic.org/editors-picks/let-suffer-love-lord/.

[42] Fr. John Hardon, SJ, as quoted in ibid.

[43] Fr. Michael Shields, "Let Me Suffer and Love with You Lord. Only with You."

[44] Pope St. John Paul II, Apostolic Letter *Salvifici Doloris (On the Christian Meaning of Human Suffering)*, February 11, 1984, n. 19, http://www.vatican.va/content/john-paul-ii/en/apost_letters/1984/documents/hf_jp-ii_apl_11021984_salvifici-doloris.html.

[45] Fr. George Kosicki, CSB, and Vinny Flynn, *Now is the Time for Mercy* (Stockbridge, MA: Marian Press, 2015), p. 82.

[46] *Salvifici Doloris*, n. 24.

[47] Kosicki and Flynn, *Now Is the Time for Mercy*, p. 82.

[48] Dan Steinberg, "Thirty Years Later, Joe Theismann Calls His Broken Leg 'a Blessing'," *Washington Post*, DC Sports Bog, November 19, 2015, https://www.washingtonpost.com/news/dc-sports-bog/wp/2015/11/19/thirty-years-later-joe-theismann-calls-his-broken-leg-a-blessing.

[49] Liberty University News Service, "Former NFL Star Motivates Crowd to Set Lifelong Goals, Live by Faith," October 21, 2016, http://www.liberty.edu/informationtechnology/index.cfm?PID=18495&MID=210350.

[50] Quoted by Fr. Jay Toborowsky, "Sheen on The Perfumed Feet," Young Fogeys blog, April 02, 2007, https://youngfogeys.blogspot.com/2007/04/sheen-on-perfumed-feet.html.

[51] Padre Pio, *Secrets of a Soul: Padre Pio's Letters to His Spiritual Directors* (Boston, MA: Pauline Books & Media, 2003).

[52] Melanie Jean Juneau, "Lord, If This Is How You Treat Your Friends ...," Catholic Mom, May 17, 2018, https://www.catholicmom.com/articles/2018/05/17/lord-if-this-is-how-you-treat-your-friends/.

[53] Fr. Roger Landry, "Revenge of the Black Toad and Miser of Souls," CatholiCity, March 5, 2010, https://www.catholicity.com/commentary/landry/00826.html.

[54] "Footprints in the Sand" (author unknown), OnlyTheBible.com, April 26, 2010, https://www.onlythebible.com/Poems/Footprints-in-the-Sand-Poem.html.

[55] Fr. William Byron, SJ, "Ask Father: Do People Who Commit Suicide Go to Hell?" *Catholic Digest*, April 1, 2007, http://www.catholicdigest.com/faith/200704-01do-people-who-commit-suicide-go-to-hell.

[56] Fr. Alessio Parente, OFM Cap, *The Holy Souls: "Viva Padre Pio"* (Edizione Padre Pio da Pietrelcina, 2011), pp. 178-79.

[57] Apparition at Fatima of August 19, 1917, "Fourth Apparition of Our Lady," EWTN.com, accessed December 7, 2020, https://www.ewtn.com/fatima/fourth-apparition-of-our-lady.asp.

Join the

Association of Marian Helpers,

headquartered at the National Shrine of The Divine Mercy, and share in special blessings!

An invitation from
Fr. Joseph, MIC, director

Marian Helpers is an Association of Christian faithful of the Congregation of Marian Fathers of the Immaculate Conception. By becoming a member, you share in the spiritual benefits of the daily Masses, prayers, and good works of the Marian priests and brothers.

This is a special offer of grace given to you by the Church through the Marian Fathers. Please consider this opportunity to share in these blessings, along with others whom you would wish to join into this spiritual communion.

1-800-462-7426 • marian.org/join

Spiritual Enrollments & Masses

Enroll your loved ones in the Association of Marian Helpers, and they will participate in the graces from the daily Masses, prayers, good works, and merits of the Marian priests and brothers around the world.

Request a Mass to be offered by the Marian Fathers for your loved ones

Individual Masses
(for the living or deceased)

Gregorian Masses
(30 days of consecutive Masses for the deceased)

1-800-462-7426 • marian.org/enrollments • marian.org/mass

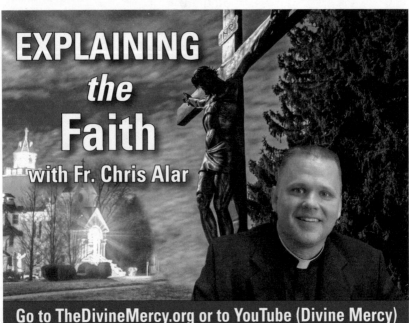

Diary of Saint Maria Faustina Kowalska:
Divine Mercy in My Soul

Also available
as an ebook —
Visit ShopMercy.org

The *Diary* chronicles the message that Jesus, the Divine Mercy, gave to the world through this humble nun. In it, we are reminded to trust in His forgiveness — and as Christ is merciful, so, too, are we instructed to be merciful to others. Written in the 1930s, the *Diary* exemplifies God's love toward mankind and, to this day, remains a source of hope and renewal. Keep the *Diary* next to your Bible for constant insight and inspiration for your spiritual growth! Also available in Spanish.

Large Paperback: Y93-NBFD   Compact Paperback: Y93-DNBF
Deluxe Leather-Bound Edition: Y93-DDBURG
Audio *Diary* MP3 Edition: Y93-ADMP3

The Divine Mercy Message and Devotion
Our most popular pocket-size handbook on Divine Mercy covers every aspect of the message and devotion. By Fr. Seraphim Michalenko, MIC, with Vinny Flynn and Robert A. Stackpole, STD. 88 pages.
Y93-M17

Divine Mercy 101 DVD
The popular presentation by
Fr. Chris Alar, MIC, is better than ever:
all the basics of Divine Mercy in a clear,
one-hour presentation. Also available as a CD.
Y93-DM102 Audio CD: Y93-NE101

For our complete line of books, prayer cards, pamphlets, Rosaries, and chaplets, visit ShopMercy.org or call 1-800-462-7426 to have our latest catalog sent to you.

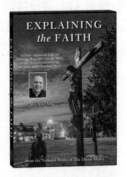
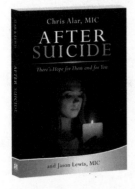